BEADING in the
Native American Tradition

BEADING in the
NATiVE AMERiCAN TRADiTiON

DAVID DEAN

INTERWEAVE PRESS
WWW.INTERWEAVE.COM

Editor: Judith Durant
Technical editor: Jean Campbell
Illustration: Ann Swanson
Cover and interior design: Susan Wasinger
Production: Dean Howes
Copy editor: Stephen Beal
Proofreader: Nancy Arndt

Interweave Press
201 East Fourth Street
Loveland, Colorado 80537-5655 USA
www.interweave.com

Printed in Singapore by Tien Wah Press

Photography credits: Cover, Mary Staley Pridgen. David Dean. Pp 24, 33-34, 36 (top), 37, 40-42, 44,
46,58, 63, 70 (top), 73, 76-78, 85, 87, 98, 112
Joe Coca. Cover, title pages, table of contents spread, pp 1, 2, 4, 7-9, 11-12, 14, 28, 32, 36 (bottom),
39, 43, 45, 55-57, 59-62, 66-67, 69, 70 (bottom), 71, 74-75, 80-84, 86, 88, 94, 100-103, 106, 109, 111

Library of Congress Cataloging-in-Publication Data
Dean, David, 1957–
    Beading in the Native American Tradition / David Dean.
      p. cm.
    Includes index.
    ISBN 1-931499-03-9
1. Beadwork 2. Indian beadwork--North America. I. Title.

TT860 .D42 2002
746.5'08997—dc21   2001059206

10 9 8 7 6 5 4 3 2

FOR MARGARET, AINSLEE, AND ADAM,
WHO HELP MAKE ALL THINGS POSSIBLE.

ACKNOWLEDGMENTS

This project started as a second thought. While teaching at *Beadwork* magazine's Bead Bash 2000, I was kind of hinting around about doing a book on appliqué beadwork. A very good friend and the editor of this book said to me, "Why not do something that is comprehensive about the common Native beadwork techniques?" After thinking about this proposal for about ten minutes, I told her I would give it a try.

Throughout this project, Judith Durant has continued to be there, working as a sounding board, editor, and more importantly, a friend. The creative director and technical editor of this project, Jean Campbell, has been working just as hard making sure that the book really looks its best and functions well. These two very special ladies are what will make this project a success. In addition, I would like to thank Linda Ligon, president and publisher, and all the folks at Interweave Press for making this book a reality. A project of this type does not just happen, it takes many hands.

After thirty years of doing beadwork, I have many people to thank. Many elders, students, and friends, most of whom grew up around the powwow circle, have taught me beadwork techniques over the years. In addition, over the past eight years or so, I have had the pleasure of teaching Native beadwork techniques in the contemporary arena. This opportunity has given me a chance to teach beadwork all over the country to people from all over the world. As a teacher of this art form, I have learned something from each student and every beadwork contact.

Finally, I would like to thank the many elders who have passed on to their greater glory. Unfortunately we may never understand their total knowledge of this art work; their knowledge has passed with them. But it is important that we continue to strive to produce beadwork at their level or even better. One day we too will become elders, and it is important that we continue to pass on the knowledge of traditional ways.

Special thanks to Ann Strange Owl Raben for granting generous access to the unusually fine private collection of the late Charles Eagle Plume. The collection is located in the Charles Eagle Plume gallery, Allenspark, Colorado.

CONTENTS

Blanket Strip. Crow style, lane stitch with running-stitch rosette. Crow Fair, Crow Agency, Montana, August 1998.

Breast Piece. Two-needle appliqué on black velvet in a turn-of-the-century strawberry design. Crow Fair, Crow Agency, Montana, August 1998.

INTRODUCTION

I've always believed that the spirit of the people can be "felt" in a good piece of work. As a young man, I spent a number of years trying my best to produce the beadwork of my heritage. There were some sources of information available; however, the instructions were either written for a child or so technical that they dealt with only the historical perspective of Native beadwork. As I began to travel and visit elders who were beadworkers, it became apparent that there was more to the story than children's projects and historical perspectives. It is my purpose with this book to give the reader a starting place not only for how to do a particular technique, but how to do further research, purchase the right tools, and understand the Native perspective on this fascinating art form. I hope I have accomplished my purpose in an easy-to-read and understandable format that will inspire you to your greatest potential as a bead artist.

Remember that this book is not the final authority. I believe that we as beadworkers will never thoroughly understand the work that we produce or take it to its highest potential. We can, however, take our beadwork to the next level and realize that as future generations begin to understand this art form, they in turn will take it to the next level. Beads and beadwork have a story much like the history of Native people—there is the past, the present, and the future. Only through the study of the past can we gain an understanding of the present; the future of Native beadwork is in the hands of the artists who will continue to produce it.

Dance Apron detail. Mesquakie-style two-needle appliqué. Wayne Wagner, 1999. Private collection.

A SHORT HISTORY OF BEADS AND BEADWORK IN AMERICA

Cape. Sunburst pattern worked in lane stitch on buckskin. This is a contemporary powwow piece; the feather motifs and sunburst outlining are not traditional, nor are they characteristic of any particular tribe.

> There is no death.
> Only a change of worlds.
>
> *Chief Seattle, Suquamish*

GLASS BEADS AND EARLY TRADING IN NORTH AMERICA

Upon the arrival of Columbus and his "discovery" of a New World, Europeans became interested in the many riches that world offered. Furs and timber were plentiful in many regions, and gold and silver were being mined and used for religious items in Mexico, where slaves could be obtained to work the mines. These and other goods held great value for Europeans. In return, the Native populations of North America were fascinated with European technology. Metallurgy, glass making, weaving techniques, and the ability to domesticate horses as beasts of burden held great value for Native Americans.

Before the Europeans arrived, many Native peoples along the coast of the areas now known as Virginia and New England traded among themselves in a product called wampum. Wampum is a bead made by hand from the quahog or hard-shell clam (*Venus mercenaria*). There are only two colors of this type of shell bead: white and dark purple. Wampum beads generally are about one-quarter inch in length and one-eighth inch in diameter. Wampum was very often strung in long strings or woven to form belts. The combinations of certain colors and designs woven in a belt could be used to send messages from tribe to tribe.

When Europeans came to North America, it was immediately clear that their money was of no value. In order to deal with the Native populations, the Europeans had to adapt to the Native barter system. Because of the success that beads had afforded the Europeans with African trade, they became the standard for trade in North America as well. And because of the way beads were packaged (in large wooden barrels), they made perfect ballast for the large sailing ships. Glass beads soon replaced wampum as the basis for European trade with Native Americans.

▪ Placing a value on goods

The value of European goods was often set by the Native populations rather than by the Europeans, and the value of many traded items was determined by the basic economic philosophy of supply and demand. Europeans soon realized that regions determined the value of certain goods. For instance, some tribes valued particular colors of beads more than others. We know the value assigned to many of the beads by looking back at records kept by the Hudson Bay Company. Because beaver hats were a fashion trend in Europe, the "made" or "plew" beaver was a prime trade good and its value was used as a common

rate of exchange. (A made or plew beaver was a beaver hide that had been scraped, stretched, and cleaned for shipment.) For example:

Green beads with white centers:
six = one made beaver
Transparent pea-size green and yellow beads:
six = one made beaver
Large amber, transparent blue, or opaque beads:
two = one made beaver
Large opaque blue beads:
one = two made beavers

From roughly 1790 to 1840, millions of beaver furs were traded and shipped to European markets.

▪ Trading venues and rendezvous

Many trading posts were located in St. Louis and in other sites along major waterways. In order to get the best price for the beaver and other furs, trade companies began sending their representatives into mountainous areas of the West where they could deal not only with Native people, but also with mountain men. The companies supplied these mountain men with the necessary equipment for trapping animals. As the men traded furs, a percentage of their value went back to the company to pay for the equipment. Some of the men were "free trappers" who owned their own equipment and traded with whomever they wished, often at a higher barter value. These rugged outdoors mountain men were typically the original explorers responsible for many of the trails that eventually became roadways across the country.

Whenever the white man treats the Indian as they treat each other, there will be no more wars. We shall all be alike—brother of one father and one mother, with one sky above us and one country around us, and one government for all.

Chief Joseph, Nez Percé 1898

Annual events, called rendezvous, offered an opportunity for trade between company trappers, free trappers, other mountain men, and Native people. Rendezvous were sponsored by large trading companies that were based in the eastern part of North America and had direct ties to European markets. The rendezvous were held close to river access so that furs could quickly be shipped back East. Items traded for the furs included beads, cookware, yard goods, blankets, rifles, whiskey, trapping supplies, and all manner of household goods. These annual events offered a place not only to trade but to renew old friendships, gamble on horse races and other games of chance, and to hold contests in rifle shooting, and knife and tomahawk throwing. The rendezvous also afforded the setting for weddings with Native women. Many marriages that took place at these events were designed to expand trading relationships and usually had little to do with love or long-term commitment. The western rendezvous was the place of high commerce on the American continent, and it was not uncommon for conflicts between Native tribes to be put on hold until after an annual rendezvous, when goods for plunder were plentiful.

▪ Seed beads come to North America

During the early nineteenth century, millions of large, wire-wound beads and lampworked beads were traded with the Native populations. Chevron, padre, melon, French cross, millefiori, and many other types of beads, including small amounts of "E" (size 8°) beads were also traded at this time.

While this trade was conducted in the West, a new, smaller bead, what we now call the "seed" bead, was being traded to bands of eastern Native people. Starting as early as 1770, seed beads were generally traded by the string or by the pound. Seed beads began making their way across the country, and the first seed beads traded in the West were the above-mentioned size 8° or E. These beads were known as pony or pound beads. The name pony refers to how the beads were transported, and pound refers to the rate of exchange. A pound of beads was worth a finished buffalo robe or a good horse.

When, in the late 1830s, traders brought large amounts of seed beads to the western plains, they were surprised to find that small amounts of seed beads had already appeared there. These beads came from the East and the South by way of the early Native trade routes and from the North via French Canadians. When the Lewis and Clark expedition made its way to the upper Northwest, members were amazed that while many of the peoples they encountered had never seen a white man, they possessed European trade goods.

THE BEGINNINGS OF NATIVE AMERICAN BEADWORK

Before the arrival of glass seed beads, most decoration by Native women took the form of quillwork, painted hides, or woven fibers. The colors that women worked with were earth tones that came from natural dyes and pigments. Although tribal people were impressed with all the colors of glass beads, blue beads in any shade seemed to be considered most valuable. Fascination with the color blue stems from the Natives' difficulty

Wearing Blanket. Contemporary Crow work in lane stitch.

in producing a deep blue from natural dyes and pigments. Reds, yellows, oranges, purples, greens, and shades of these colors were relatively easy to produce. In addition, many Native women considered having beads in light shades of blue like owning a "piece of the sky." Therefore, as trade values were established, blue beads of any shade generally had a higher value than other beads.

In many pieces of early Native American beadwork, it is not unusual to find only two or three different colors of beads. This in many instances stems from the lack of other colors available at the time the work was done. As a way of increasing the value of other colors of beads, many traders would trade in only a few colors. By creating a false sense that a certain bead color was hard to come by, they could raise the price. In addition, many traders had enough space to deal in only a limited number of beads.

▪ Treaties

Between the 1860s and mid-1880s, treaties were reached between the federal government and many Native tribes, and annual allotments of goods became standard treaty terms. Treaties generally included provisions for goods such as cloth, staple foods, fresh meat, farm implements, hunting weapons, household goods such as knives and kitchenware, and, of course, beads and blankets. As the treaties were put into practice, the Bureau of Indian Affairs (BIA) was established and charged with overseeing the terms of the treaties. The BIA created

Indian Agencies to supervise the distribution of provisions. In addition, trading posts were established for commerce between Native people and the local white population. Beads and blankets were standard trade goods, and they were traded with Native women for things like finished beadwork, tanned hides, moccasins, and other Native products. Again, the economic philosophy of supply and demand determined the price of a pound or string of beads.

▪ Tribal craft guilds and designs

After the mid-1870s, most Native people were relegated to reservations. Ironically, this is also the time when beadwork production reached an all-time high. There are a number of reasons for this surge. First, giving up the life of a nomadic people afforded many Native women the time to produce craft work for pleasure. Second, the availability of beads at local trading posts exploded. Along with more time and beads, craft guilds sprang up in many tribes. The guild was an important place for young girls to learn good beadwork skills. For a lot of four- and five-year-old girls, helping their mother or grandmothers sew and bead a doll was their first bead project.

This important involvement established a girl's place in the society to which she was expected to conform, and the guild became the place where new techniques and designs were exchanged. Acceptance for membership in guilds varied from tribe to tribe, but most girls were expected to belong to a guild at some time in their lives.

> Beadwork, like all art, is a mental process. The difference between the work's being craft or art is how much the creators of such work are willing to give of themselves. Beadwork can be a Craft of the Mind or an Art of the Soul.
>
> *David Dean*

Many guilds operated informally, somewhat like quilting bees. The guild gave women a sense of belonging and a place to keep informed about tribal events and to exchange the latest gossip.

Eventually, producing beadwork became a way for Native women to hold on to their Indian identity. To the Native way of thinking, a design belonged to the person who created it. Designs could be owned by an individual, a family, or a guild. An individual's design could be copied as long as appropriate payment for its use was made to the owner. Designs recognized as property of a certain family could only be used by members of that family. Designs that were developed by guild members were usually property of the guild, and they became the designs most frequently used by their tribe. Over time, designs were shared as tribes developed relationships with other tribes. Some of these relationships were in the form of marriage, since most tribes did not stand alone but would intermarry with another tribe that they considered friends. Through these relationships, shared designs were sometimes slightly changed to create a new design.

■ European education for Indian children

As the reservation system took hold, many Indian children were sent to Indian schools. These schools were established as part of treaty agreements, and European education was considered of prime importance. Many schools were boarding schools that housed children from a number of different tribes. Handwork of all kinds was taught by the missionaries who operated the schools, and it included many forms of European-style beadwork. While Native people had previously developed their own beadwork techniques, many of the skills taught by Europeans were adapted to fit the Native way of thinking and style of decoration. Traditional Native designs and color concepts learned from elders merged with the newly acquired European handwork techniques. Students practiced their skills using large quantities of beads distributed by the schools. As the skills of these students grew, local posts traded finished pieces for beads and other supplies.

BEADWORK AS COMMERCE

In the early 1890s, a small group of ethnologists and collectors began to accumulate beaded items for museums and their own private collections. In order to fill the needs of a particular collection, it was common for a collector to provide the necessary materials to the person making the item and then purchase the completed beadwork.

After the Dawes Act, or the General Allotment Act of 1887, which allotted tribal lands to individuals and effectively broke up the system of communally held tribal lands in Oklahoma, small towns sprouted up around the former reservations. Many towns had stores that carried supplies used by Indian people to make dance clothes and create goods for a new tourist market. Americans had begun to travel on vacations, and now, throughout the west, in towns and on reservations, it became common to see Native people selling their beaded pieces from roadside stands. This industry provided the means for many Native people to feed their families. As a result, much of the Native beadwork produced from the early 1900s until the end of World War II was nothing more than tourist curiosities.

■ Native beadwork post–World War II

At the end of World War II, there was much excitement in the Indian community as the "new warriors" returned home from European and Pacific theaters. In Native American culture, warriors are revered as people deserving the utmost respect and honor. Powwows and other gatherings were organized to honor the returning veterans, and this was a time in history that Native people were at once proud of their heritage and proud Americans. There was a great resurgence in Native culture. Powwows

> As beadwork is created, a rhythm is established. The consistency of the rhythm is what lets the artist create great art. If broken by not consistently doing beadwork, the rhythm must be re-established in order to produce quality work. For this reason beadwork should be done every day. Start by doing only thirty minutes a day. As your ability and creativity mature, increase the time you bead every day to an hour.
>
> *David Dean*

became commonplace, and there was a dance going on almost every weekend of the year.

With the revival of Native celebrations came the need for beadwork to decorate the clothes for powwow. In addition, a larger body of serious collectors of Native materials appeared, willing to pay good prices for quality pieces of beadwork. Some beadworkers began to enjoy a reputation among these collectors as artists, and for the first time in Native history, beadwork began to be looked at as art rather than craft.

Pride in Native heritage continued to develop throughout the 1960s and 1970s, and more powwows and Native gatherings began to spring up across the country. With this resurgence of Native pride came new styles of beadwork. As cars and planes made it possible for Native people to travel to Indian gatherings both near and far, tribal beadwork styles became increasingly blurred, and a new style developed called Pan-Indianism. This style of beadwork blended a number of different styles and, for the most part, obscured tribal identity. Beadwork became identified with regional areas rather than tribal style.

In the 1980s and early 1990s, many Native people and others who studied Native culture began to study old tribal styles of beadwork. This investigation has resulted in a renaissance of many of those styles. In Indian country, it is still possible to find the occasional trading post that sells beads to Native customers, and among them an

old stash of beads may be discovered. Beads are also traded and sold at Native gatherings and through mail-order catalogs. These authentic materials help the contemporary beadworker to replicate traditional beadwork.

New styles are being developed among contemporary Native artists, and they exist alongside the historical and traditional beadwork styles. Native beadwork is today, as always, in a state of change, perhaps now more than ever. Many changes are due to the availability of Japanese beads and the learning of new techniques. But the largest reason for change today is the willingness of the artist to step outside the conventional bead box and break some of the rules that traditional beadworkers have clung to

for years. Traditionally, beadwork was not produced unless there was a specific use for it. This beadwork could include dance clothes, religious items, or items that could be sold to help support a family or tribe. Today it is common for Native beadworkers to produce beadwork for beadwork's sake, for the art of the work. As this concept grows, items are being made as art objects rather than for utilitarian purposes. It is common today to find Native artists making wall hangings, beaded jewelry, beaded contemporary clothing, and accent pieces to be worn with contemporary clothing. And who knows? Fifty years from now, what is considered very contemporary by today's standards may be considered traditional.

Hard-soled Moccasins with bell anklets. Contemporary work, probably Sioux, in lane stitch.

RESEARCHING NATIVE AMERICAN BEADWORK

Cuff. Crow. Lane stitched borders
with Crow stitch interior patterns
and zipper edge on red wool.
Charles Eagle Plume collection.

The study of Native American beadwork is
no different from that of any other topic in
at least one respect—in order to understand
what direction we are currently going in, it
is important to understand where we have
been. Familiarity with historical beadwork
designs and methods gives us a firm foun-
dation for the development of new techniques and helps us to think outside the box
when we create beaded items. Moreover,
many people who would like to own a piece
of antique beadwork find the cost prohibi-
tive. One solution is to create new pieces
using old techniques, designs, and colors.
Any contemporary beadworker can be an effective scholar of items created over one
hundred years ago. Many traditional techniques may at first appear to be very simple.
However, when you consider the tools used
and the quality of materials available at the
time, it becomes apparent that the creation
of beadwork in the 1800s was no easy matter. And in addition to an artistic eye, the
artist had to have creative ingenuity.

WHERE TO START

Many people begin to study antique Native
American beadwork with the thought of
recreating a particular piece. It is important
to realize that by studying only one piece of
work you will have only the insight of the
artist who created that piece. In order to develop a sense of what a tribal style really looks
like, you must study a number of pieces from
the same tribe, created during the same time

Pipe Bag. Crow, c. 1850. Lane stitch worked
on buckskin with wool trim and zipper
edge. Charles Eagle Plume collection.

period. Close observation is the best tool you have as a student of Native American work. The most obvious things to note when you look at beadwork include the techniques, the color and types of beads, the type of thread and other materials, and the common designs on a number of pieces of beadwork.

Some Cheyenne beadwork at first glance appears to be created in lane stitch, while in reality it may be stitched in a technique called Cheyenne loop stitch. The difference in appearance between lane stitch and loop stitch is subtle; the humps in rows of loop-stitch work are less pronounced than in lane-stitch work. But the actual methods of producing the two are very different.

▪ Color and design

Color and color combinations are also critical elements for establishing what tribe produced a particular piece of work. Many tribes were partial to particular colors of beads. To many contemporary beadworkers, the color combinations used by Native people don't seem to go together. By careful study of the colors and color combinations used in different pieces, one can learn which ones represent established tribal preferences. Some tribes were very specific as to colors used; other tribes used almost any color available.

Designs or motifs are the next thing to consider when you are studying historic beadwork. Some designs have no meaning to anyone other than the person who beaded the item, but almost all designs were *tribal* specific. Most nineteenth century tribal people lived in partnership with other nearby tribes and many of these tribes would intermarry. It was common to find Sioux, Cheyenne, and Arapaho families intermarried. Upon close examination of the beadwork designs produced by each of these tribes, you can see that many designs are almost the same, with only very subtle differences distinguishing one tribe's work from that of another.

▪ Dating beadwork

The date is the next critical thing to consider when you are studying Native beadwork. Since it takes about twenty years for a new technique to become established and used on a daily basis, you should consider studying beadwork in twenty-year increments. Styles of beads and other trade goods changed frequently; if a study period is longer than twenty years, you run the risk of missing certain refinements in materials and techniques. As the technology of bead making improved, new techniques evolved, different sewing threads were introduced, and the use of needles became commonplace. It is important to learn when certain types of beads were produced and when they were imported to North America.

In the early days of beadwork production by Native people, many used thread made of sinew (long tendons from large animals such as buffalo or elk). As other thread became available, first linen and then cotton, it replaced sinew. Needles also changed how beadwork was produced. Crude iron needles, and later steel needles, replaced bone awls. However, around the turn of the twentieth

When a man does a piece of work which is admired by all we say that it is wonderful; but when we see the changes of day and night, the sun, the moon and the stars in the sky and the changing seasons upon the earth, with their ripening fruits, anyone must realize that it is work of someone more powerful than man.

Chased-by-Bears,
Yankton Sioux 1910

century, many collectors requested that sinew-sewn beadwork be produced to add to their collections. Moral of story: "Just because it is sinew-sewn does not make it old." The distinguishing sign that shows that a piece is in fact old is how the hole was made in the hide that the beadwork is sewn on. In later pieces of sinew-sewn beadwork, the sinew thread was sewn with a needle. In earlier pieces, the holes were made with an awl and no needle was used.

STUDYING MUSEUM COLLECTIONS

Again, the best way to get a good understanding of Native American beadwork is through close observation of actual pieces. Unfortunately, not all of us have Grandma's trunk full of old beadwork in the basement to look through. Museums have become my Grandma's trunk. Almost every museum in America has a number of Native pieces in its collection. Most museums see it as their purpose to provide a place for scholars to do research, and curators are usually very helpful about giving the serious student access to their permanent collections.

It is important to understand protocol when you are working with museums. First, develop a letter of introduction explaining what you are seeking to do. A letter sent in advance of your actual visit will help open the door to your adventure in the museum. Be sure to call ahead and make an exact appointment time with a curator. Remember that some collections are very old and must be handled only while wearing gloves, and in some instances the pieces can't be handled at all. Be sure to ask if it is okay to take pictures of the pieces you are studying. Because the bright lights involved with flash photography can harm many fragile items, you may be able to take pictures only without a flash. Be sure to ask the curator's assistance in handling pieces.

You should also be aware that the data associated with museum collections is not always accurate. Many times the data on a particular item is the information given to the museum by the person who donated the piece. This source leaves a lot of room for error, since the person making a donation may know little or nothing about the piece. For example, Uncle Mike was a collector of Native American antiquities. After his death, no one in the family knew what to do with the collection, so they decided to give the collection to a local museum. Unfortunately, Uncle Mike was not a great record keeper, so there is now little or no accurate information accompanying the pieces. The curator is not a scholar of Native collectibles so he labels a particular piece as a Cheyenne pipe bag when in fact it is of Arapaho origin. This mistake is easily made because Cheyenne and Arapaho work are very closely related. It may take an expert in the field to distinguish between the two tribal styles. Many times the mistakes made in museum collections are much more obvious. By no means am I saying that all information in museums is unreliable, but it is important for the serious student to realize that the problem of misidentification does exist.

If for some reason it is not possible for you to visit museums, the next best thing is to study their catalogs. Many museums

Blanket Strip. Sioux, c. 1870. Five-bead lane stitch, sinew-sewn on buckskin. Charles Eagle Plume collection.

Doll Carrier. Chippewa, c. 1875.
Appliqué on black wool.
Charles Eagle Plume collection.

publish and sell catalogs of special exhibits to help defray the cost of the shows. These catalogs include photos of the pieces in the show. The advantage to this method of study is that a piece can be revisited time and time again. In addition, many museums sell slide sets of their collections.

OTHER AREAS OF STUDY

Another avenue for the study of old beadwork is through photographs taken of Indian people before 1920. Many interesting designs and techniques can be discovered in these photos. It is best to study field photographs as opposed to those taken in a studio. Many props used in studio photography belonged to the photographer, not the person being photographed, and this practice may lead you to draw wrong conclusions. It is not uncommon to find photos in which the tribal pieces being worn are of mixed origin. For example, you may assume that if you are looking at a photo of an Osage man, everything he is wearing is Osage when in fact certain items may be Sioux, Crow, or Blackfoot. Between 1880 and 1905, photographer John A. Anderson of South Dakota took photos of at least eight different Sioux men, each wearing the same Blackfoot bonnet, holding a Cheyenne bag, and wearing Crow leggings. Only through careful identification of each piece can the appropriate identifications be drawn.

Over the years, many studies have been done on Native American beadwork. Some studies were done by government agencies, such as the Smithsonian Institution's Bureau of Ethnology. Each year from the late 1870s to the 1920s, the Bureau sent an ethnologist into the field to live with Native people and study their tribal traditions and living conditions. Each year the field ethnologists issued reports to the head of the Bureau on what they had studied. Bureau of Ethnology Reports discussed not only daily living habits of Native people but also addressed other aspects of life including decorating techniques. In fact, *Beads and Beadwork of the American Indians* by William C. Orchard was originally published as a Bureau report. There have also been numerous magazine articles published about Native culture. Unfortunately, many of these articles are now out of print and hard to find; however, they are important resources. Some magazines to look for include *American Indian Tradition, American Indian Hobbyist, Whispering Winds, Moccasin Tracks, Powwow Trails, Singing Wire, American Indian Craft and Culture,* and *American Indian Art.*

You can also see lots of Native beadwork at events such as powwows. Native gatherings can be a very satisfying way to study Native beadwork because you can often talk with and learn from the artists and master craftspeople who created the pieces. Don't be shy about asking questions. Most beadworkers enjoy talking about their craft and great friendships can

We were taught to believe that the Great Spirit sees and hears everything, and that he never forgets; that hereafter he will give every man a spirit-home according to his deserts. This I believe, and all my people believe the same.

Chief Joseph, Nez Percé

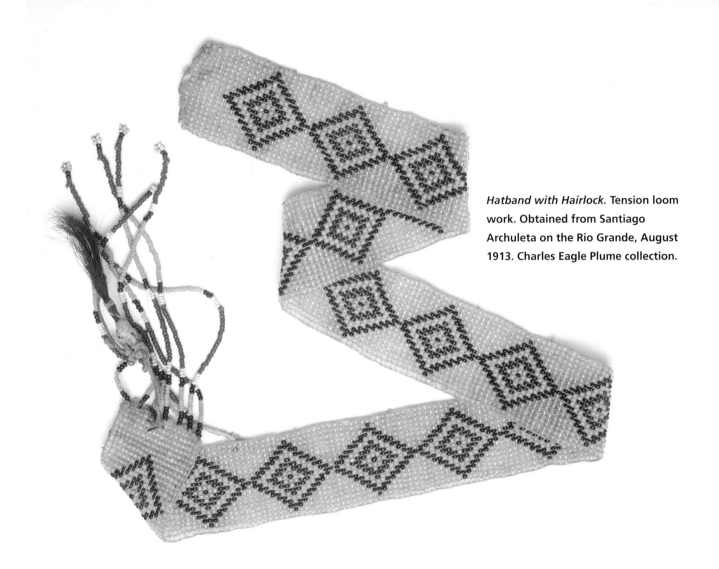

Hatband with Hairlock. Tension loom work. Obtained from Santiago Archuleta on the Rio Grande, August 1913. Charles Eagle Plume collection.

be developed this way. However, due respect is the key for successful study using this technique. Never photograph a piece unless you first ask the owner. Small gifts to older folks such as tobacco or a hank of beads may be the key to getting them to open up and talk about their work. By listening closely, you can learn many things about how a piece is put together and why it is done a certain way. The wisdom imparted by these folk may be the most valuable information you can obtain. But remember that no one person can speak for an entire tribe or all Native people.

Information about local Native gatherings can be obtained by contacting Native American organizations or chambers of commerce, and they are often listed in local community calendars.

TECHNIQUES FOR ACCURATE STUDIES

Your study of Native beadwork and culture will be more enjoyable if you have the proper equipment. You'll need a pad of paper and good quality colored pencils to sketch designs. A good camera is a worth-

while investment for taking pictures of the pieces you are studying. Remember to check museum policy or ask the artist's permission before snapping photos. For studying photos, a good magnifying glass or cartographer's glass will be helpful. Good measuring devices are essential for the study of Native beadwork. Use a six-inch ruler, a tape measure (cloth is best when examining old pieces), and an outside caliper.

As your study of Native work grows you will develop a keen eye for detail. Many details that give pieces their "Native look" are very small and easily missed at first glance. Always note size of beads, techniques, colors, patterns, and construction details. Many pieces produced between 1880 and 1920 were sewn together on treadle sewing machines. Do not assume that a piece is hand sewn simply because it looks so. Careful study is the key to accuracy.

Take notes on 4" × 6" index cards. The information should include type of article; tribal affiliation; age of piece; technique(s) used; type and colors of beads, thread and other materials used; artist if known; location of the piece (where it was found or where it currently resides); and measurements of the piece. Insert this information, along with a photo of the piece if available, into a plastic photo sleeve and file it for future reference. Establish a good filing system to make your research easily accessible. You may arrange your data by technique of beadwork, type of article, or tribal affiliation.

OTHER STUDY CONSIDERATIONS

Many pieces of beadwork found in museums are part of old medicine or religious bundles. Respect should be paid to these pieces and while it is okay to collect photographs of them, they should never be reproduced in beadwork. Religious and medicine bundles hold special meaning for tribal people, and many of these pieces are currently being repatriated to the tribes that originally owned them. When you're studying Native beadwork, take the time to understand what you are observing. Just as you would not want someone who is not of your faith treading on objects that you consider sacred, that same respect should be paid to these items. Only through careful study can you understand the differences between religious and sacred items and those used on a daily basis. This type of study requires that students surround themselves with scholars and resources that they can trust. When in doubt, ask your trusted source and remember: There are no dumb questions.

Finally, the study of old beadwork can open up a new world for your beading adventure. It gives you the chance to look at other cultures and understand how items from another culture developed; gives you technical information; and broadens your knowledge of beads and their impact on the world.

BEADWORK RESEARCH CARD

Date Made _____

Technique(s) _____

Type and Color of Beads Used _____

Thread and Other Materials Used _____

Artist _____

Location _____

Measurements: Length _____ **Width** _____ **Diameter** _____

COLLECTING NATIVE AMERICAN BEADWORK

As with anything of value—art, craft work, or any other collectible—education will lead to the best collection. You should know as much as possible about what you are trying to collect. This education can take a number of paths: formal education, powwow education, book and research education, and education given by Native people. There are very few places to get a real formal education. But if you are going to be a consumer, you must know what you are consuming.

Decide what your Native American beadwork collection will include and assess your knowledge of that area. There are a number of different styles and tribal differences. Are you going to collect historical or contemporary pieces? How much do you know about the techniques involved? How much do you know about the raw materials involved? What is a fair market price for a piece of Native art? These are just a few of the questions that must be considered by the serious collector of Native American beadwork.

BEADWORK STYLES

The following is a description of basic beadwork styles and some thoughts on what makes a particular piece of beadwork "good." Remember that a number of tribes may do the same style of beadwork, and the clues to tribal identification can often be found in the colors and designs employed. You may encounter other styles of beadwork, but they can generally be associated with one of these categories.

▪ Lane stitch or lazy stitch

Lane stitch is one of the most widely used styles of beadwork done by Native Americans. It is characterized by rows or "humps" of beads sewn down to buckskin or canvas. There are generally seven to eleven beads sewn in a stitch or lane. The best work is done on brain-tanned, smoked buckskin. A good substitute is commercial tanned elk hide. Canvas is also used for certain kinds of work that have a tendency to get wet or sweat-soaked. Good lane-stitch beadwork has a hard feel to it, with little movement of the lanes in a row. This type of beadwork is used to make large pieces because the work can be done quickly.

Lane-stitch beadwork was generally done by tribes on the upper plains, west of the Mississippi—the Cheyenne, Sioux, Arapaho, Kiowa, Crow, and other Great Plains tribes. In many historical pieces, the work is sewn with sinew (long tendons from large animals like deer and buffalo). The hard feel of lane-stitch beadwork is accomplished by filling the holes of the beads with as much thread as possible and pulling the stitches of each row very tightly.

▪ Cheyenne loop stitch

Cheyenne loop stitch is a variation of lane-stitch beadwork, with the beads in all rows but the first sewn down only on one side. The other side of the row is looped around the threads of the row just below it. Loop stitch tends to have a flatter look than lane stitch, but it should have the same hard feel. This loop variation was done almost exclusively by the Southern Cheyenne tribe. As with lane stitch, the best work is done on brain-tanned hides, and older work may be sinew sewn. Both these types of beadwork are probably the most common historically and were among the

Don't be afraid to ask bead dealers if the price they are asking is their best price. Generally the larger quantity you buy, the cheaper the beads.

David Dean

first techniques learned by Native Americans for using beads as decoration.

■ Heddle loom work

Heddle loom work is used to produce the large flat pieces of beadwork generally associated with tribes of the upper Missouri River area. As in the weaving of fabric, in heddle loom beadwork a heddle is used to raise alternate warp threads so the weft, which carries the beads, can pass through and be locked into place. Used historically to produce large bandoleer bags, this type of loom work is a common technique among the Winnebago, Potawatomi, Oto, Iowa, and Mesquakie tribes. Good work has an even edge with very little wave. This type of work is not very common in the marketplace and therefore generally brings a high price for good examples.

■ Tension loom work

Tension loom beadwork is used to produce large flat pieces in a woven type of fabric. Tension loom work is smoother than heddle loom work and less thread is visible in the finished piece. In tension work, the threads are strung on an upright loom to create a warp into which beads are woven. This is a fairly modern technique and few pieces exist that were made before 1900. Good work has an even edge and should be backed with a good material. Tension loom work is simple and fast to do, and a large amount has been imported from Japan and other countries over the years.

NATIVE AMERICAN BEADWORK STITCHES

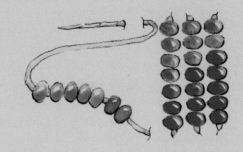

Lane stitch

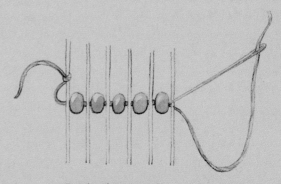

Cheyenne loop stitch

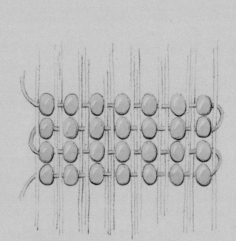

Heddle loom work

Tension loom work

NATIVE AMERICAN
BEADWORK STITCHES

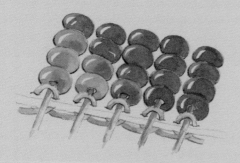

Crow running stitch

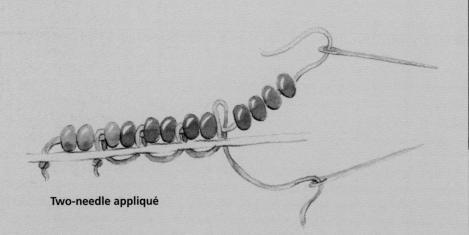

Two-needle appliqué

▪ Crow running stitch

An appliqué stitch, Crow stitch is generally done with two needles; the first thread strings the beads and the second thread tacks the first thread down every few beads. The number of beads tacked down at one time on a given piece may vary from three to six to ten. Due to the fact that so many beads are tacked down at one time, work done in Crow stitch tends to have some movement to it, and it is characterized by rounded corners and wavy lines. Crow stitch is common on the upper plateau regions of the country and is done frequently by the Crow, Blackfoot, Nez Percé, Yakima, and other tribes of Montana, Idaho, and Washington. The technique is used to make large pieces of beadwork such as rifle cases, shirts, and dress tops. The best work is done on brain-tanned buckskin or tightly woven wool cloth. Crow-stitch work has a bumpy appearance.

▪ Two-needle appliqué

Two-needle appliqué is a variation of Crow stitch. It involves two needles, the first one stringing beads and the second one sewing down every two beads. This type of work can be used to achieve complex patterns in which bead placement is very exact. The technique is in popular use by tribes in the Missouri River Valley and the eastern United States, including the Iroquois, Sac, Fox, Iowa, and Potawatomi. Good work has a tight feel with little or no movement, and it's done on wool, buckskin, canvas, and canvas weave materials like mending fabrics. It is common to find two-needle appliqué done on a backing material with the pieces cut out and sewn to a larger article such as leggings, wearing robes, and blankets. Good two-needle appliqué work will lie flat and will not cup or have a dome shape; this happens when the beads of each row are sewn too close together. This is the technique used to create "picture" bags common to tribes in plateau regions of the country.

▪ Return stitch

Return stitch is an appliqué technique that uses one needle. Two beads are strung and sewn through backing material. The needle is then brought back between the beads and strung back through the last bead. This technique is very effective when exact bead placement is necessary, as in the production of geometric rosette designs, and it's found in a great deal of Oklahoma-style beadwork.

▪ Gourd stitch

Gourd-stitch work is found on small beaded pieces such as fan handles, dance canes, rattles, and small dangles attached to large clothing pieces. The technique forms a woven net of beadwork that "floats" on top of a base. In general, good work is done in small beads, size 12° or smaller. Gourd-stitch work is characterized by bold color combinations in geometric patterns, with the best work done in a "three-drop" style. Three-drop uses a mathematical progression based on the use of symmetrical designs created with bead counts of three or six beads in each design element. Gourd-stitch work is done extensively by the

NATIVE AMERICAN BEADWORK STITCHES

Return stitch

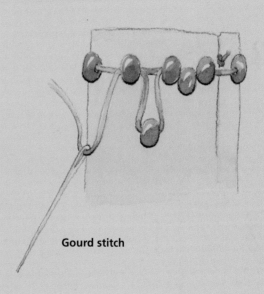

Gourd stitch

Remember that beadwork is heavy. It is best to store completed pieces lying flat. This keeps the hanging pressure of the glass from pulling on the beadwork threads.

David Dean

NATIVE AMERICAN
BEADWORK STITCHES

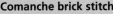

Comanche brick stitch

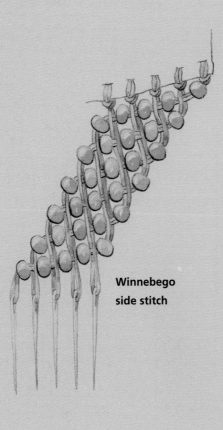

Winnebego side stitch

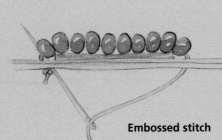

Embossed stitch

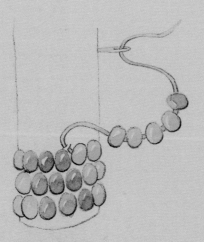

Wrapped stitch

Kiowa, Comanche, Ponca, and other Oklahoma-based tribes. All the very best work is done on objects covered with buckskin.

▪ Comanche brick stitch

Comanche brick stitch is used in the same way as gourd stitch. The beads stack up like the bricks on a house, hence the name. Good work uses smaller beads, generally in symmetrical designs. This type of work is done almost exclusively by the Comanche and Kiowa tribes, with the very best work backed with buckskin or other soft leathers. Brick stitch and gourd stitch can be distinguished by the direction in which the beads lie on the piece. In gourd stitch, the bead holes lie horizontally. In brick stitch, the beads lie like bricks on a house, with the holes positioned up and down.

▪ Winnebego side stitch

Side-stitch beadwork is possibly one of the most complex stitches used by Native American beadworkers. It can best be described as finger weaving with beads. Used by tribes of the upper Midwest, it is commonly found on objects such as garters, ladies' hair ties, armbands, and other places where small flat pieces of work are needed. Good work will lie flat and won't twist or have bulges.

▪ Embossed stitch

Embossed, or raised, stitch is practiced among the tribes of the upper northeast: the Iroquois, Seneca, Mohawk, and Canadian Cree. The stitch is applied to geometric or pictorial patterns on small items created for the tourist trade. The patterns stand out in strong bas relief from the wool, silk, or taffeta they are worked on. The relief effect is achieved by using large E to pony-sized beads, by padding the pattern areas with paper (whose color tends to show through the beads, which are typically translucent), and by crowding the beads in their allotted space.

■ Wrapped stitch

One of the simplest of beading techniques and among the first developed by Natives, the wrapped stitch is used to cover small-diameter cylindrical objects such as cords and fan handles. The object to be wrapped is first covered in buckskin. The thread is secured with a small knot through the buckskin, and twelve to fifteen beads are strung and wrapped around the object. A backstitch through the last bead holds the wraps in place, and then more beads are strung. Wrapped stitch can be found on early pieces from most tribes.

FACTORS THAT DETERMINE GOOD BEADWORK

Many factors determine whether a piece is a good example of a certain type of beadwork. Considerations include the following.

- Is the work historical or contemporary in origin?
- Is the material base the best available for the time in which the piece was constructed?

- Was bead selection a priority in the construction of the piece? (The best beadworkers sorted their beads, discarding uneven, cracked, or chipped beads.)
- Does the work have the right "feel" for its style?
- Do tribal factors play a part in the style?
- Is the artist well known or the student of a well-known artist?
- Are threads used in the piece coated with some sort of thread dressing such as beeswax? (Beeswax helps alleviate wear on thread and is desirable in beadwork.)
- If it is an historical piece, do the beads and materials reflect the time period in which the piece was made?
- If a piece is identified with a tribe, does it in fact employ a common tribal design and technique?
- If it is an historical piece, does it have beads or sections of work missing, or has the piece been stabilized to preserve its historic value?
- What price for a similar piece was paid at recent auctions, by collectors or galleries?
- Generally, fully beaded pieces are worth more than partially beaded pieces.
- Is the piece considered to be a collectible and in high demand?
- Generally, pieces beaded with smaller beads are worth more than pieces beaded with larger beads.

- Are the beads used in the piece cut beads or antique beads?
- Is the piece made from legal animal parts? (Depending on when the piece was made, federal and state game laws must be considered when feathers, furs, and claws are used.)
- In historical pieces, do wear marks appear where one would expect them to?
- What was the original intended use of the piece? (In historical work, was the piece used as clothing or for religious purposes or was it made for the tourist trade? In contemporary work, was the piece built as art or as dance clothes?)
- Are you dealing with a reputable dealer or artist?
- Do you like the piece?
- Do you have a basic understanding of how the piece was made? Were standard technical procedures followed?
- Will the piece be functional for its intended use?
- Is good solid hardware used in the piece? (For example, if the piece is a hair barrette, are the barrette attachments of good quality?)
- Does the builder of a piece offer any type of guarantee about its construction?
- Don't be fooled by stories or lines about the real intended purpose of a piece. Research is the best resource when you're considering historical pieces.

- Is the piece complete? (For example, if you are considering a knife sheath, is the knife included? Complete pieces are worth more. This is true for both historical and contemporary pieces.)

- With contemporary work, it is important to get to know the artist if at all possible and be aware of the different types of work that he or she may do.

- Many times beadwork is only part of a much larger piece; it is therefore important to be aware of other craft forms such as hide work, ribbon work, and work done with hair and feathers.

- Documentation is a must with historic work. Recording date collected, who collected it, from what tribe it was collected, and as much information as possible about a particular piece may be helpful in determining its value.

- When you're collecting contemporary work, get a piece of paper signed by the artist that says how the piece was constructed, why it was constructed, and any other information that might be of value in future sales of the piece.

- Be aware that re-creation of historical pieces is a fairly easy thing to accomplish. If something is supposed to be over a hundred years old, it should appear to be over a hundred years old.

- Historical reproduction is maybe the best way to collect historic pieces. There are artists who specialize in historical reproduction.

- The true value of contemporary work may take a number of years to come to resolution. Good contemporary work will always go up in value.

PREFERRED TRIBAL COLOR CHOICES

As beadwork developed on the North American continent, many tribes came to prefer certain colors and color combinations. While there is no exact record of color preferences, and while many artists worked in the colors at hand, the list below can serve as a guide to common techniques and colors used by specific tribes.

This is just a starting point; beadworkers might use any color available. The specific time in history that a piece was made will have some bearing on the colors used.

TRIBE	TECHNIQUES	PRIMARY COLORS USED
Sioux	Lane stitch, appliqué	White, red, navy blue, green
Crow	Crow stitch, appliqué	Pink, light blue, yellow, white
Cheyenne	Lane stitch, loop stitch	White, red, green, yellow, dark blue, light blue
Arapaho	Lane stitch	White, red, green, navy blue
Nez Percé	Appliqué	White, light blue, brown, green, red
Yakima	Appliqué	White, blues, greens, browns, red, orange
Blackfoot	Appliqué, lane stitch	White, green, red
Mesquakie	Heddle loom	Green, light blue, white, amber, pink, navy blue
Kiowa	Appliqué, gourd stitch	White, red, orange, yellow, turquoise, navy blue, green
Chippewa	Appliqué, heddle loom	White, green, clear, transparent, reds, oranges
Comanche	Gourd stitch, single lanes of lane stitch	White, brick red, green, yellow

New beads were introduced from time to time and they found a niche among certain groups. The Cheyenne tribe was particularly partial to cut beads when they first became available.

CREATING AN "ARTIFAKE"

An artifake is a reproduction of a Native piece that is designed to copy a particular style of beadwork. With the high value placed on original pieces of historical Native-produced work, artifakes represent an alternative way to produce and collect historically significant Native beadwork. *Artifakes are not created to be sold as originals.* However, some of the aging techniques discussed here can produce an original patina. Only unscrupulous dealers will try to sell an artifake as an original. Collectors purchasing Native beadwork must take care to deal with only reputable dealers.

The reasons for production of artifakes are many. First and foremost is the cost of owning an original. A reproduction can cost thousands less. Second, reproductions can be beautifully created and include areas and parts that might be missing from an original. Third, reproductions can be handled and used, unlike their original counterparts. Fourth, there is a challenge involved in the re-creation of an historical piece of beadwork. This challenge lies not only in the reproduction of the technique, but in finding the right materials, and studying the work in question. The study of the piece alone can be an adventure in knowledge acquisition. Successful reproduction of an historical piece of Native American beadwork is 90 percent studying of style, technique, design, and color, and 10 percent actual work. Only through a detailed study can all the secrets of a particular piece of beadwork be brought to light.

▪ Aging a new piece of beadwork

Once you have done your research and produced your beadwork, how do you add a patina suited to the time frame you are trying to replicate? First, you must do an overall study of the completed piece. In this process additional parts may be added such as tin cones, trim dangles, or other appropriate trim work. Once you have determined the structural aspects of the piece, remember that over time tin will rust, and any trim will have a worn appearance. To re-create natural aging, soak tin in lemon juice to cut any oil on the metal. Soaking cones in a saltwater solution adds a dulling film that in a few weeks turns to rust.

Experimentation with small awls and hole punches will help the re-creation artist in duplicating small bug holes and wear marks associated with the original. It is important to realize that in original work dirt and dust play a major role in the creation of patina. With many pieces of historic work, what gives the piece an old look is the dirt that shows between the beads. Quality dirt and dust must be added to duplicate the original. Simply vacuuming your house can make museum-quality dirt. Carefully remove the bag from an upright vacuum and cut the bag open. With a makeup brush, dab dirt and brush it into the beadwork. Be careful not to add too much dirt, only what will make the piece match the original. If you use a large quantity of beeswax when you're building the work, the dirt will adhere more readily to the beads.

With many older pieces of work, larger trade beads give the piece a finished look. Many of these beads have a dull finish due to their use and wear over the years. Soaking new trade beads in a solution used to etch glass can duplicate the older finish and wear. Care must be taken not to leave the beads in the solution for too long, however, or the acid will eat away at them. It is a good idea to check the beads every twenty minutes or so. Remember that you want to just eat away the shine.

Check the original for wear marks left by consistent use. If your pipe bag doesn't have wear marks, grab one and carry it as a pipe bag would be carried. The high surfaces should have a natural layer of dirt and the lower spots should be cleaner and less used. Some items made of buckskin need to be stretched. Do so by soaking the desired area in alcohol and pulling the hide in all directions as the alcohol evaporates.

Good work will always command a high price. Remember that as an historical reproduction artist, you spend 90 percent of your time identifying how something was put together over a hundred years ago and figuring out how to re-create a hundred years of age.

TOOLS, MATERIALS, AND HOW TO BUY BEADS

As with any artistic endeavor, choosing the right materials for the project is critical to its success. Fortunately for beadworkers, the tools and materials used, other than beads, are not many and may already be in your craft stash. Historically, the basic tools used by Native people were very minimal and included an awl, sinew, brain-tanned hides, beads, and in the latter half of the nineteenth century, thread and needles.

As with beadworkers today, Natives had many ways of storing their supplies, and almost all produced storage bags. Many bags were works of art, decorated with all kinds of beadwork. Among the Southern Plains peoples, it was common for a woman to carry a knife, an awl, and some needles on her belt. These tools were the primary instruments for preparing hides. Knives were used to skin and scrape the hides, and the awl and needles were used to sew up holes that resulted from shooting and butchering the animal. A Native woman kept these items close at hand while doing her daily chores. Similarly, the contemporary beadworker should have tools designated as "beadwork" tools and

Dance Canes and Fan Handles. Kiowa-style designs worked in gourd stitch. David Dean, 1980s. Collection of the artist.

should keep them in a place reserved for beading supplies and projects.

LIGHTING

The most important tool for a beadworker is good light. Even beadworkers with fine eyesight depend on light to help them produce quality work. In days of old, most beadwork was done in the light of day to insure proper production, and the best lighting is still natural. If you have the opportunity to design your own work space, large windows placed high on the north wall will provide a consistent, full spectrum of natural light.

There are several lighting options for beadworkers. Lamps with high-watt incandescent bulbs are best, but they can create high heat. Fluorescent lights can be good to work with because they offer a fair spectrum of light yet give off very little heat. Halogen lamps are another alternative, but they, too, produce a lot of heat. Full-spectrum lights such as those offered by Ott are a good choice; the bulb is fluorescent so little heat is given off. Experiment with different lamps in combination and figure out what works best for you.

In addition to type of light, lamp

placement is critical when you're working with beads. Place the lamp in a position that focuses the most light on the work without throwing shadows.

AWLS AND NEEDLES

Made from a buffalo shoulder or leg bone, traditional Native awls were often the only tool used for beadwork; they punched holes in soft buckskin through which sinew could be threaded to attach beads. In some tribes, crude needles were also fashioned out of bone. As technology and trade improved, iron and steel awls became commonplace among Native people, and when iron and steel needles were developed, they became the preferred tools for doing beadwork. Unlike current practice in our disposable society, Native women would use a needle until there was nothing left to work with. If the tip of the needle broke, it was routinely resharpened and used until it could no longer be sharpened. Special cases to store needles were built not only to protect a needle from damage but also to prevent it from being lost.

Today beadworkers have a variety of needles and awls to choose from. With improvement in metallurgical technology, tempered awls and needles are readily available and represent valuable tools for all craft workers. Awls used in leatherwork can be used to produce beadwork on leather. You may also create an awl by gluing a handle to a large leatherworking needle. See the sidebar below.

Needles come in a variety of styles and sizes; the higher the size number, the smaller the needle. Needles most commonly used for beadwork come in two styles. First are loom needles that range in length from two to three inches. The other style needle is called a "sharp" or "short" needle due to its length and is used for off-loom techniques. There is also a needle on the market called a "Big Eye"; here the eye runs almost the whole length of the middle of the needle and collapses as the needle is used. The "twist" needle is good for stringing large beads and pearls. You may also encounter long beading needles that range in length from ten to twelve inches. These needles are used in bead factories to string beads into hanks.

The most common needle sizes are 10, 12, 13, and 15. When you're selecting

HOW TO BUILD AN AWL

One of the most important beadworking tools is a good metal awl to punch holes in hide and to use as a pick to sort and separate threads. Old dental instruments make good picks for moving thread; they can also be turned into awls with the addition of a larger handle.

One of the simplest awls is made from a number 6 or 8 leather-stitching needle. These needles are unique because they are not round but triangle shaped. The edges of the needle actually cut, rather than pierce, hides, and make them easier to sew through. To construct the awl, use a small piece of dowel rod with a hole drilled in the end. Glue the needle into the hole. Other choices for handles include drawer pulls, which can be found at almost any hardware store. The handle should be comfortable in the hand and easy to hold on to. Epoxy glue is the best for gluing awl tips into handles. It is important to keep an awl sharp. A small triangle file can be used for this purpose. Do not heat the awl when sharpening or the temper will be drawn from the metal and make the tip brittle.

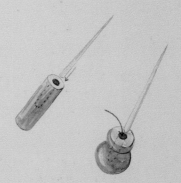

Make an awl with a drawer pull or dowel rod and a leather-stitching needle.

USING SINEW AS THREAD

Split sinew using an awl tip.

To make a needle point, wet the sinew, twist it between the thumb and forefinger to form a point, and allow the sinew to dry.

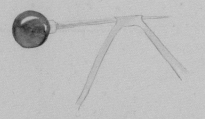

Bend the leather to insert awl tip.

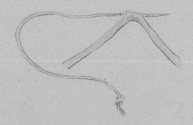

Knot the sinew and pull it through the hole.

needles, it is important to choose a size compatible with the size of beads you're working with. Generally, the size of the needle should match the size of the beads. In addition to beading needles, the maker of Native-style beadwork should have many different sizes of leather needles.

THREAD

Originally, threads used by Native people were made from plant fibers or sinew. Plant fibers were braided or twisted into thread by a number of different methods. Because this thread tended to be somewhat thick, it was used with large beads. Sinew was prepared when an animal was killed for its meat.

To prepare sinew for threading beads, first scrape the sinew to remove all the fat, then dry it slowly in the sun to create a piece of material approximately three by fourteen inches. Once dried, the sinew has the consistency of stiff rawhide. To form thread, pull small strips of the fiber from the sinew sheet. Soak this stiff thread in water; once thoroughly saturated, it can be used to sew or string beads. In the past, much sinew-sewn work was done without the aid of a needle. To use sinew without a needle, soak the tip of the sinew and twist it into a needle-like end. Allow the needle end to dry and become stiff. Before stringing or sewing beads, soak all the sinew but the dry needle tip in water.

To attach beads to hide, punch holes in the hide with an awl and poke the sinew through the holes.

The major drawback to using natural threads is that they attract bugs that will eat them. This is true of both sinew and plant fibers. The problem can be minimized by storing pieces of beadwork in cedar boxes or boxes with mothballs. Some Native people also used horse tail-hair as thread. Beadwork produced with horsetail usually was worked without a needle and is mainly found in pieces of diagonal weave done by tribes of the upper Midwest.

Europeans introduced linen, silk, flax, and cotton threads to the Native population. As trade increased, many women switched from Native-produced threads to European-produced threads. All the above-mentioned threads are made from natural fibers and tend to rot over time. Coating the threads with beeswax increases their life spans. Beeswax also helps keep thread from tangling and aids in threading it into needles. Much of the beadwork held in museums that dates to the early 1860s is constructed using cotton quilt and button thread. As technology changed, threads were produced from synthetic fibers. Made in different sizes, these nylon and polyester threads also found their way into the production of Native beadwork.

Today we have a number of choices for creating beadwork. Each thread available today has its own pros and cons. Polyester is the best choice for heddle loom work because it has very little stretch. Many traditional beadworkers still use cotton coat and button thread for lane-stitch beadwork. Nymo thread is good for gourd stitch and appliqué beadwork due to its strength-size ratio. High-tech threads such as kevlar and silamide have not been used in Native work long enough to predict whether Native beadworkers will continue to use them.

The best thread for general use seems to be Nymo well-coated with beeswax. Nymo comes in different sizes, and it is important to choose the size thread that goes with the type of beads and beadwork you are producing. Beads in the 13° range and smaller can be worked with size A, 0, 00, and 000 sized thread. Larger beads can be worked with size B, D, E, and F thread.

BACKING MATERIALS FOR NATIVE WORK

The material of choice for traditional beadwork has been and continues to be either brain-tanned buckskin or fine woolens of the type handled by early traders. Brain-tanned buckskin is conditioned rawhide—if it gets wet, it will quickly turn stiff. To keep buckskin soft and pliable, the hides are routinely smoked. Smoking closes pores in the hide to keep it supple, and also adds color to white tanned hides. Smoking also shrinks hide, so it is important to stretch smoked hide before using it. To stretch a hide, tack the top to a large piece of plywood or other flat surface. Spray the hide with water, pull in all directions, and tack it down along the edges. Once the hide is dry it is ready to work with. By

following this stretching process, you can expect to gain about nine more inches of usable size from a full hide.

Tanned hides were smoked by being hung in the top of tipis, close to the smoke hole. On the southern plains, hides were typically not smoked as heavily as hides in the North, probably because the winters were shorter. The shorter smoking of southern hides produced buckskin of a lighter color. Color of hide was also determined by the kind of wood used to smoke it. Southern hides would be shades of light brown or tan, northern hides were dark tan to almost chocolate color.

Commercially tanned hides can be substituted for brain-tanned hides and are more accessible to most beadworkers. The major difference between brain-tanned hides and commercially tanned hides is the removal of the scarfskin with the hair from brain-tanned hides. Without the scarfskin, the brain-tanned hide appears to be suede on both sides. When you're purchasing commercial hides, look for evenness. Hides should not be too thick in some areas or too thin in others. When you're producing work on commercially tanned hides, work on the flesh or suede side to give the finished product a Native look. Thin elk hides are good for sewn beadwork. Currently a number of companies are producing a brain-tanned look-alike hide. These hides are suede on both sides and come in colors that match smoked hides.

Very tightly woven wool fabric, used to make military uniforms of the day, was a

common trade item during the 1700s and 1800s. Like many items traded to Native people, wool quickly became a material to decorate with beadwork. Many woolens had a woven selvedge to prevent the cloth from raveling. This selvedge was often of a different color, the most common being black, navy blue, or scarlet red. Native people often worked this selvedge into a piece of clothing to make it multicolored. Much appliqué beadwork was produced on this type of fabric.

Canvas can be used as a substitute for buckskin. The difference in technique when working with canvas is that the needle is brought all the way through the fabric; with buckskin, the needle goes only halfway through the hide. Canvas can be a good backing material for beadwork that is to be worn, such as for dance clothes. Canvas takes sweat and moisture better than buckskin.

Velvet was a common backing material with eastern tribes, and it was often backed itself with brown paper sacks.

Today there are a number of fabrics that can be used to back Native beadwork. Generally, you want a material that will allow beads to stand up evenly. Two pieces of mending fabric with typing paper ironed in between makes a good backing material for a lot of beadwork. Layers of canvas sewn together also make a good stiff backing. Wool is still a good choice for prairie-style beadwork, which uses curvilinear designs. The wool is easy to work with and is historically correct.

SCISSORS AND CUTTING TOOLS

As their main cutting tool, Native bead-workers generally used knives that were first built from chipped flint and later made of iron or steel. Most beadworking knives were small, with blades less than four inches long. This same knife was used to skin and dress hides, cook dinner, and perform many other daily chores. As scissors became a common trade good, Native beadworkers quickly understood this tool's ease and convenience. Overnight, the simple scissors became one of the hottest items offered by European traders. Unlike European women, Native women used their scissors over and over, sharpening them repeatedly until they would no longer function.

The types of scissors produced today have made beadwork easier than ever before. Micro-point scissors and good leather shears are key to producing Native-style work. Even if you need to cut corners when buying equipment, never underestimate the value of good scissors. Have your scissors sharpened regularly and oil the joint occasionally. These two procedures alone will prolong the life of your best scissors for years.

In addition to scissors and shears, a good razor knife is hard to beat for cutting threads extremely close, cutting out appliqué work, or finishing the edge of a rosette.

One of the best tools to come along in the last few years for cutting hides, cloth, and other types of bead backings is a roller

Trays of beads for sale at the Crow Fair, Crow Agency, Montana. August 1998.

knife. These knives have replaceable blades and, when used with a straightedge and cutting board, can make a perfectly straight cut. This tool is most valuable for cutting buckskin or ultrasuede into fringe. It is wise to keep an extra blade on hand because they do wear with continual use.

PLIERS

Although not historically used by Native beadworkers, a small pair of pliers is an essential beadwork tool. Pliers can be used to break beads from the thread as they are strung—if you string too many, or an incorrect size, it is easier to break the offending bead(s) than restring the whole lot. Small ignition pliers used for automobiles work well and fit easily in your beadbox. Pliers can also help attach buckskin to solid objects like fan handles. Glue the buckskin down with white craft glue, then pinch the seam with pliers where the ends of the buckskin come together.

NEEDLE CASES

Native women made small cases for needle storage, generally of hard leather or rawhide decorated with beadwork. Today, one of the first projects you may want to bead is a needle case. You can use a turned wood needle case, an old pencil lead case, or almost any type of small container. A small metal box with a magnet strip stuck to the inside lid makes a great needle case.

BEESWAX AND THREAD CONDITIONERS

∎∎∎

Native beadworkers have used beeswax since they began to do beadwork as an art form. Not only does beeswax keep thread from tangling and raveling, it fills up the holes in the beads and keeps them from moving around in the completed work. When you're buying beeswax, smell it to determine the honey content. The stronger the honey smell, the better the wax.

A number of thread conditioners have been invented to replace beeswax. Some are good, some are not so good. I still use beeswax. Many people complain that beeswax compromises the look of the finished piece by adhering to the beads. You can avoid this buildup by spraying a soft cloth with window cleaner and gently rubbing your finished beadwork. This treatment removes not only beeswax but fingerprints and body oils from the completed beadwork and makes the beads sparkle.

BEAD STORAGE

∎∎∎

As you carry on your journey with beads, particularly if you become a "power buyer," you will undoubtedly find storage of these little spheres of glass a problem. Many people store beads in plastic tubes, small medicine bottles, or any variety of small containers. For years, I have routinely stored my beads in plastic peanut butter jars. My jars each hold a half kilo of beads, which is more than most people

will buy. Native women stored beads in small, easily portable bags made of buffalo bladders or scrotums. Most Native beadworkers did not keep a large stash of beads, preferring to trade for them as needed. Another traditional Native way to store beads was in small pine needle baskets with tight fitting lids. There are many storage gizmos on the market today, and the key to efficient bead storage is finding a system that works for you.

BEADS AND HOW TO BUY THEM

∎∎∎

The history of the beads used in Native American beadwork is of great interest, and being able to identify the type of beads used becomes very relevant when stabilization or reproduction work takes place. (Stabilization is work done to stop or slow the aging process on beadwork held in museums.)

∎ Italian seed beads

The Italians, originally on the island of Crete and later on the mainland, developed the first seed bead production facilities. Historically, Native people traded for Italian seed beads, which were typically finished by hand. Long glass tubes were given to women in a cottage industry who cut them to size and finished them by hand, placing them in a keg with sand and slowly turning the keg over a fire. The hot sand worked as a polishing agent. Because they were finished by hand, old Italian beads tend to be very uneven, and sorting out misshapen beads was a typical process in the creation

of Native work. For very fine pieces of Native work, sorting was one of the most important production processes. The Italians used a different bead sizing nomenclature than what we are familiar with today. An Italian size 4° bead is approximately the same size as a Czech size 12° bead. An Italian size 5° is about the size of a Czech 13°. Italian bead production stopped during World War II and Italian beads are now considered antiques. Italian beads came in softer colors than Czech beads, and it is common to find Italian beads with a purple or blue hue that results from the glass-making process.

In addition, many Italian colors had a "greasy" hue, and the names that these beads eventually became known by were often determined by that trait. Greasy yellow, sea foam green, and greasy blue are just a few color names for popular Italian beads. The Italians also produced the first white lined or "white heart" beads, invented to make colored glass go twice as far. White or clear glass was used for the center and then the bead was dipped in colored glass.

Italian beads were generally packed in bulk and not on hanks as Czech beads are. Italian beads are sold by weight today, usually by the ounce or pennyweight. Some colors of beads weigh more than others because of variation in the weight of the metals added to produce the colors. Adding gold to glass produces red, adding copper produces green, adding aluminum produces blue.

▪ Czech seed beads

As bead technology spread throughout Europe, the Czechs became the leading producers of beads traded in the Americas, particularly after 1890. Czech beads generally are bolder in color than their Italian counterparts. The Czechs took bead technology one step further than the Italians did by mechanizing manufacture. As a result, the beads became more uniform in shape and size, and sorting Czech beads, which tend to be somewhat donut shaped, is not critical.

Czech bead sizing is based on how many rows of beads it takes to equal one inch; if it takes eleven rows, the bead size is 11°. The smaller the bead, the more it takes to make the same length, therefore the larger the size number. Common Czech sizes are 10°, 11°, 12°, 13°, 14°, 16°, 18°, and 20°. Any bead smaller than a size 13° is considered a fine, petite, or micro bead. These small beads were not produced after World War II, so like Italian beads, they are now considered antiques.

The Czechs were the first to produce cut beads in large numbers; cut refers to beads that are faceted. The flat cut portion is polished to give the bead a flash or sparkle. Most commonly you will find three-cut or tri-cut beads. Charlotte beads, usually available in size 13°, have a cut on only one side.

The Czechs were also the first to use the hank as a measurement for sale of their product. Most non-cut beads are sold in a hank that has twelve 12-inch loops. Charlotte beads are generally sold in hanks of twelve 6-inch loops.

▪ French seed beads

While most beadwork produced by Native beadworkers has been made with either Italian or Czech beads, French beads have often been used when Italian beads were not available.

The French began bead production to fill the niche left vacant by Italian bead makers after World War II. Many Italian bead makers never recovered from the devastation of the war, so the French met the demand for the colors of beads that the Italians had produced. The French also produced white heart beads in the same manner as the Italians had, and they became the major suppliers of lined beads.

The French figured out how to put a very large hole into a very small bead, and size 16° French beads can be used with a size 13 needle. French nomenclature differs from the Czech, and French beads are usually a little larger than their Czech counterparts. Usually a 13° French bead will be comparable to a 12° Czech bead.

▪ Japanese seed beads

When the Japanese entered the market, bead making took on a whole new dimension. Japanese bead makers computerized the mechanical process used to make glass beads, and the result is a bead that, shape-wise, is possibly the most perfect bead produced. The boxy, squared shape of Japanese seed beads is different from those produced by the Italians, Czechs, or French. Many Native beadworkers will comment that Japanese beads are too perfect and that part of the Native look comes from the use of the more oval Czech beads. The Japanese have also developed beads called Delicas and hex beads. Delicas are more cylindrical than spherical, and hex beads are almost like small bugle beads.

Because Japanese beads come in over 500 colors, it seems that these are *the* beads to work with. However, in order to make so many colors, many Japanese beads are painted or dyed, whereas a red European bead is made from red glass. As finished beadwork is used, the color begins to wear off Japanese beads; for this reason, most Native beadworkers avoid them.

Japanese beads are usually sold by weight. They generally run about one full size larger than Czech beads; a size 11° Japanese bead is comparable to a size 10° Czech bead.

Always try to buy enough beads of the same color to finish any project you are working on. Beads, like thread, come in different color or dye lots. Once you get halfway through a project, it may be almost impossible to find the exact color you are working with.

One of the most important pieces of advice I have heard in my years of doing beadwork is from George Barth, author of *Native American Beadwork* (Schneider Publishing, 1993): "Know your beads."

▪ Estimating the amount of beads needed for a project

One of the toughest things to do is to figure out how many beads you need for a project. Use the following formula to calculate the number of beads per square inch. This formula uses Czech beads as the standard.

1) Measure the length and width of your planned project in inches. Multiply the two numbers to get the number of square inches to be beaded.

2) From the following table, select the size beads you will be using.

10° = 130 per square inch

11° = 187 per square inch

12° = 228 per square inch

13° = 272 per square inch

3) Multiply the number of beads per square inch in your selected bead size by the number of square inches in your planned project to get the total number of beads needed.

4) The following table gives the approximate number of beads per hank.

10° = 3,100 per hank

11° = 4,000 per hank

12° = 4,500 per hank

13° = 5,000 per hank

Select beads per hank for the size bead you will be working with and divide that number into the total number of beads needed for your project. Round up to a full hank number. This formula works for hanks of twelve 12-inch loops. Cut beads generally come in 6-inch hanks, so be sure to double the amount when buying them.

For example, let's assume you are using size 11° beads and your project will measure six by ten inches.

6 × 10 = 60 square inches (size of your work)

60 × 187 = 11,220 beads (number of beads needed)

11,220 divided by 4,000 = 3 hanks, rounded up to a full hank

Based on your design, now estimate the proportion of colors you are planning to use. You will need at least one hank per color. However, in the example used above, if half the beads are to be white, you will need two hanks of white.

BEAD SIZING

By understanding bead sizing scales, you can use different beads from different makers on the same piece of work. Use the following chart of bead sizes to compare beads from each country of production. A key point to remember is that the larger the number used for a bead, the smaller the bead.

Bead Size Comparison Chart

Italian	3°	4°	5°	6°		
Czech	11°	12°	13°	14°	16°	
French	12°	13°	14°			
Japanese	12°	13°	14°	15°	15° hex	

When you use this chart, remember that it is a rough comparison. Cut beads have a tendency to be about one size smaller than the number indicates. As technology in glass making progresses, only time will tell what the next new seed bead will look like in both color and size.

LANE-STITCH BEADWORK

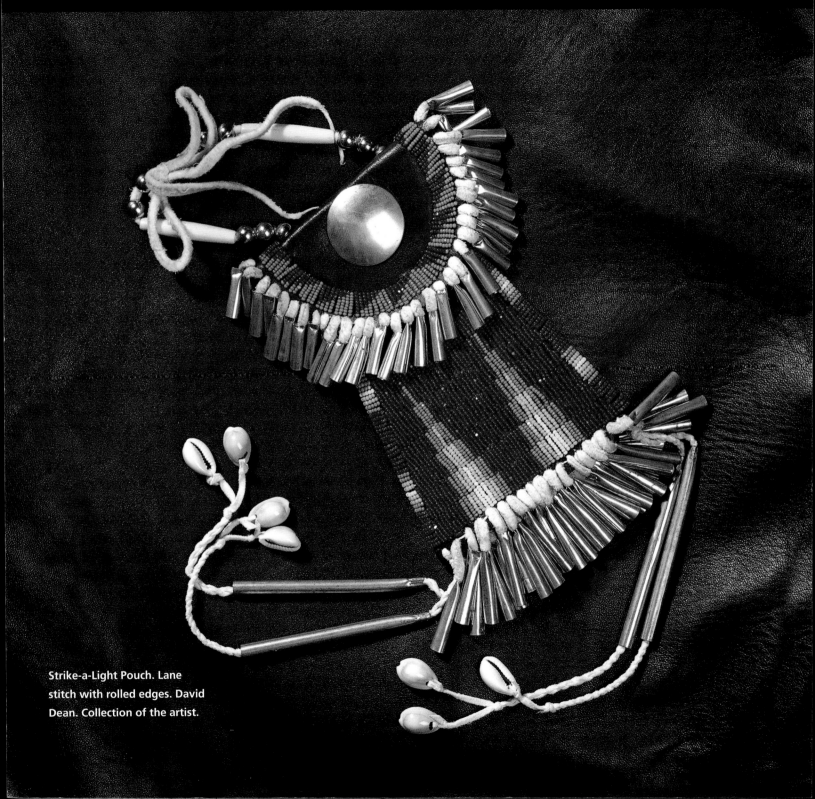

Strike-a-Light Pouch. Lane
stitch with rolled edges. David
Dean. Collection of the artist.

One of the earliest techniques used by Native beadworkers was the lane stitch or lazy stitch. Lane stitch consists of lanes or rows of six to ten beads that are anchored at each end. Native beadworkers developed this style of work without influence from Europeans. Lane-stitch beadwork was always done on brain-tanned hides, and older pieces used sinew thread, usually from buffalo or elk. Most all tribes on the Great Plains used the lane stitch in one form or another, and it is uniquely Native American. Many of the designs produced in lane stitch follow those seen in quillwork or parflèche painted pieces (parflèche is a French word that means rawhide case).

First, the sinew is prepared by separating it into strips of a size that will pass through the beads. The end of the sinew is then totally saturated with water or saliva. The tip of the thread is rolled between the thumb and index finger until a point is formed. When this end of the sinew is allowed to dry, it becomes hard, with the consistency of rawhide. The hard tip becomes the needle used in the work. Before it is used, the remainder of the sinew thread is totally saturated with water or saliva.

For lane-stitch work, an awl is used to punch holes halfway through the top layer of the hide, but never all the way through. The beads are then strung and the sinew threaded into the hole. Good quality lane stitch work feels hard or solid because the holes in the beads are filled with as much sinew thread as possible. As each stitch is made, the thread is pulled very tightly.

Doctor's Bag. Sioux-style design worked in lane stitch. The chalk-white background is characteristic of this type of work. Tim Monaghan, 1999. Collection of the artist.

SIOUX-STYLE LANE STITCH

On buckskin: sew halfway through the hide.

On canvas: sew all the way through the fabric.

Punch hole, string beads, thread sinew through hole.

Sew beads in lanes.

Not enough thread.

Fill up the holes in the beads with thread.

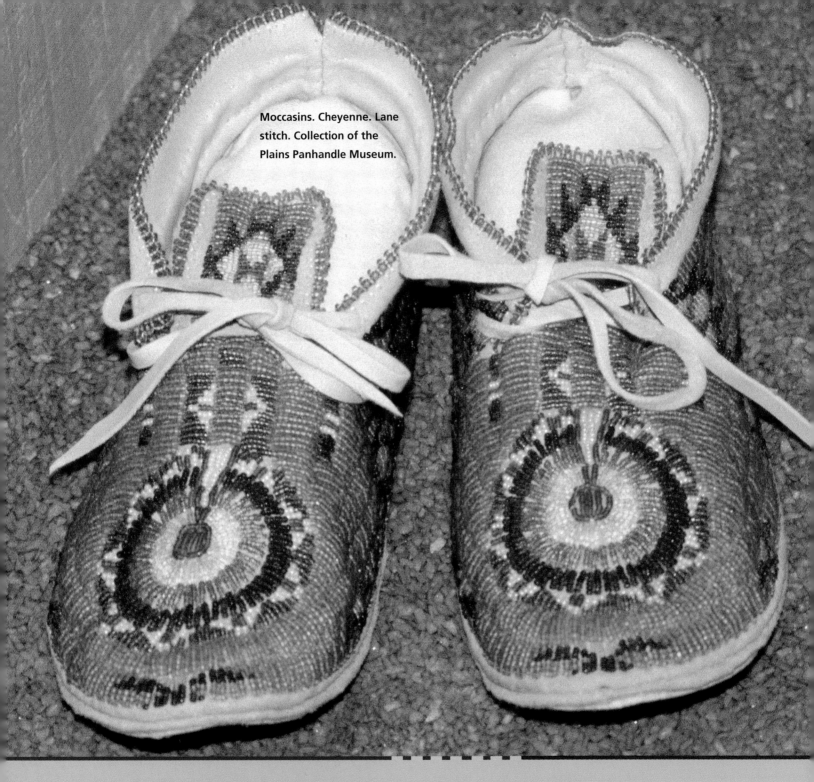

Moccasins. Cheyenne. Lane stitch. Collection of the Plains Panhandle Museum.

I have seen that in any great undertaking it is not enough for a man to depend simply upon himself.

Lone Man, Teton Sioux

When the sinew dries, it pulls the stitches even tighter.

▪ Sioux-style lane stitch

As lane-stitch beadwork developed, two very distinctive styles emerged—Sioux-style lane stitch and Cheyenne-style loop stitch. Sioux-style work can be easily identified by the obvious humps that form in the lanes of the work. In fact, the Sioux name for this stitch *is* hump stitch. The beads in each row are a bit crowded and the number of beads sewn into each row determines the arc or hump. For example, eight beads are worked in a space the size of seven and a half beads. In Sioux beadwork, the lanes typically measure one-half inch or wider. Again, the hard feel of good work is accomplished by filling the bead holes with as much thread as possible. This means that, today, larger threads such as Nymo D or F should be used doubled. For Sioux-style lane stitch, always use the largest size of thread possible so there is no unfilled space in the bead hole.

When you're working this stitch on hide, it is important to pull as much of the stretch out of the hide as possible in order to insure that the work does not pull in the wrong direction. (See the tools and materials chapter for hide stretching techniques.) Once the hide is dry, it can be used to produce beadwork.

After you decide on the design, the next step is to lay out the lanes of the work. This is best accomplished by drawing the design on a piece of paper and imposing lanes over the design; refer to this drawn design while working with the beads. Establish a baseline by marking the hide with a pencil and laying masking tape along this line. Once you establish the baseline, measure up one-half inch and use a second piece of masking tape to mark the outer line of the lane. Never mark on a hide with ink because it is almost impossible to remove.

Once you've marked the lane, thread a needle with double thread and tie a knot in the end. Anchor the thread into the hide at the edge of the marked baseline. String enough beads onto the thread to cover the lane (the space between the marked lines). Then string one extra bead to create the hump that is the hallmark of Sioux-style work. Now make a stitch at the edge of the second marked line. Needle placement is critical to successful lane-stitch beadwork. As you add each row, take a large enough stitch so that the rows are not bunched together, but not so large that the backing material shows through the rows. When the stitch is done properly, the beads in one row will just touch the beads in the next row. Once you complete a lane, remove the tape and measure one-half inch over. Use a piece of masking tape to mark this next lane.

SIOUX-STYLE LANE STITCH

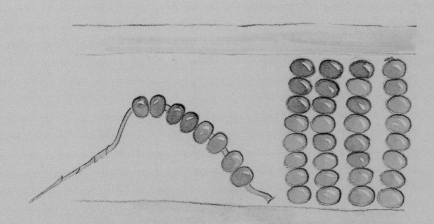

Lanes are generally one-half inch or less in width. Mark the hide lightly with pencil and then lay down strips of masking tape to define lanes.

Beads spaced too far apart.

Beads spaced too close together.

Beads spaced just right.

35

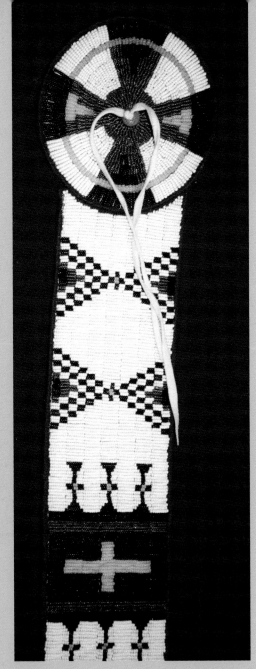

Blanket Strip. Sioux-style design, worked in lane stitch. Don Drefke. Private collection.

Bladder Bag. Probably Sioux. Lane stitch with quill-wrapped fringe, feathers, and dangles. Bags fashioned from buffalo bladders and scrotums were often used for bead storage. Charles Eagle Plume collection.

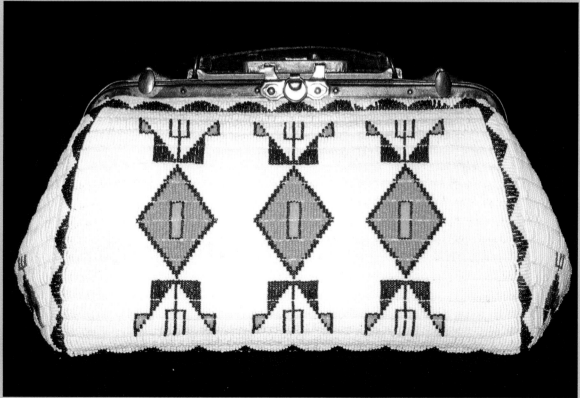

Doctors' Bags. Sioux-style designs worked in lane stitch. Tim Monaghan. Collection of the artist.

CHEYENNE-STYLE LOOP STITCH

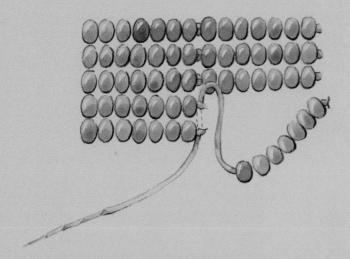

Sew the first lane down as for Sioux-style lane stitch. This lane should be sewn with as little hump as possible.

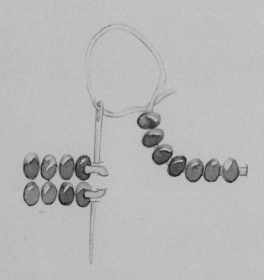

Sew thread halfway through the buckskin and loop under the stitch of the previous lane.

▪ Cheyenne-style loop stitch

Cheyenne-style loop stitch is a variation of lane-stitch beadwork. This stitch was originally developed by the band of Cheyenne located in Nebraska, on the southern plains of Colorado, in Texas, and New Mexico. The major difference between this stitch and Sioux-style lane stitch is that the obvious Sioux humps do not exist in the Cheyenne technique. A finished piece of loop-stitch work is almost flat. Most beadworkers who spend a lot of time producing work with the loop stitch claim that it is much faster than Sioux-style lane stitch.

The first lane of Cheyenne loop stitch is done exactly as in Sioux-style work except that you do not crowd the beads; you use only the number of beads in each row that will precisely fill the lane. As in Sioux-style work, it is important to use as much thread as possible to fill up the bead holes. Each row of the first lane is stitched to the hide on both sides of the lane. The rows of all subsequent lanes are stitched to the hide on the far side of the row, but when stitching to the near side, the thread is looped under the stitches of the rows in the previous lane and into the hide. When the stitches are pulled tight, the rows line up exactly with the rows in the previous lane. This exact alignment of rows is the hallmark of Cheyenne-style work.

Although Cheyenne loop stitch can be done with sinew, it is probable that the stitch developed after the introduction of needle and thread to the Native population. This is supposed because of the difficulty of looping a stitch under the previous row without the aid of a needle. Cheyenne-style loop stitch is found on many large pieces such as dresses, vests, cradle boards, and moccasins. Although the stitch was developed by the southern Cheyenne, this tribe also produced a lot of beadwork using Sioux-style lane stitch. When you're doing research, it is important to realize that tribal identity cannot be determined by technique alone.

LANE-STITCH DESIGNS

Many designs used to create Sioux-style work are also used in Cheyenne loop stitch, but the tribes use different colors. (See Preferred Tribal Color Choices on page 22.) The Sioux and Cheyenne were and continue to be neighboring tribes, and frequent intermarriage is the major reason for the similarity of design.

Lane stitch evolved in four distinct time periods and styles. The first time frame goes from approximately contact (1790) to about 1860. During this time, techniques for working beads were just starting to develop. Many designs produced in this first phase follow old quillwork or parflèche designs. The latter were painted onto the hide with pigments made from clays and plants found in the areas that these tribes inhabited. Many parflèche designs were simple block and geometric patterns; most have very few colors, and chalk white is the predominant background color. The designs are characterized by

The old Indian teaching was that it is wrong to tear loose from its place on the earth anything that may be growing there. It may be cut off, but it should not be uprooted. The trees and grass have spirits. Whenever one of such growths may be destroyed by some good Indian, his act is done in sadness and with a prayer for forgiveness because of his necessities.

Wooden Leg, Cheyenne 1889

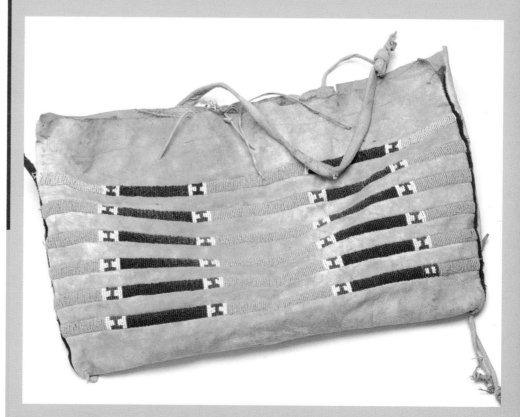

Bag. Cheyenne, c. 1870. Worked in lane stitch on buckskin with red wool piping. Charles Eagle Plume collection.

Sioux-style Pictorial Vest.
Lane stitch. Tim Monaghan,
mid 1990s. Private collection.

Sioux-style Pictorial Vest. Back view.

Sioux-style Pictorial Purse. Lane stitch with rolled edge. David Dean, 2001. Collection of the artist.

Moccasins. Cheyenne-style design worked in lane stitch. Wayne Wagner, 1999. Collection of the artist.

Color and color contrast can be as dramatic as the most complex design.

David Dean

elements that fill the entire row in a lane—very few designs start in the middle of a row. The primary reason for this is the inconsistency of the bead shapes. While simple and uncomplicated, many parflèche designs are very elegant.

The second lane-stitch design phase lasted from about 1840 to 1870. While many of the same block elements were used, new lines and smaller, more complex designs began to emerge. Designs with small lines and triangles, and designs that change in the middle of a row became common. As designs grew more complex, more color was added. Newly available smaller and better-quality beads were used. It is also during this time period that the Sioux, in particular, began covering many articles of clothing and items for daily use in beadwork. While chalk white remained the predominant background color, powder blue, turquoise blue, and turquoise green were used on occasion. Many designs from this phase became very tribal-specific as beadworkers began to employ tribal color preferences. Certain tribes began to repeat distinct designs over and over. Sioux beadworkers, for example, usually stuck to the older, more traditional block designs, whereas Cheyenne beadworkers began to experiment with color and smaller, more intricate design elements.

The third phase of lane-stitch beadwork started about 1850 and ran past the turn of the century. This design phase was characterized by more complex geometric designs, the use of border designs, and the development of pictorial beadwork. Some common designs included warriors on horseback, meetings between Europeans and Native peoples, running horse

**Strike-a-Light Bag.
Cheyenne-style design
worked in lane stitch.
David Dean, 1997.
Collection of the artist.**

designs, and battle scenes. While the Sioux were developing pictorials, many other tribes that used lane stitch began to develop extremely complex geometric designs. The background color continued to be predominantly chalk white with occasional use of blue and green. The Cheyenne began to use cut beads to create many of their outstanding moccasin patterns.

The fourth lane-stitch design phase goes from about 1940 to the present. These designs demonstrate almost all the above-mentioned elements, including bold geometric designs and pictorials, with some new and different twists. The most common distinction is the use of two techniques in the same piece, as in recent work whose beading designs are done in an appliqué technique and whose background is filled in with lane-stitch. Mixing the two techniques means that work can be done much faster. Backgrounds feature almost any color available, and many pieces seen on the dance ground today are done in these techniques.

When you're designing a piece of lane-stitch beadwork, it is important to consider the way the lanes will be set up. Historically, lanes generally run along the horizontal axis of the work. Moccasin lanes usually run around the toe for one or two lanes and then change direction and run from the top of the foot toward the toe. Lane direction can best be understood by studying old Native pieces. In some contemporary pieces, the lanes run along the vertical axis; while such lane placement is not traditional, it does make an interesting piece of work.

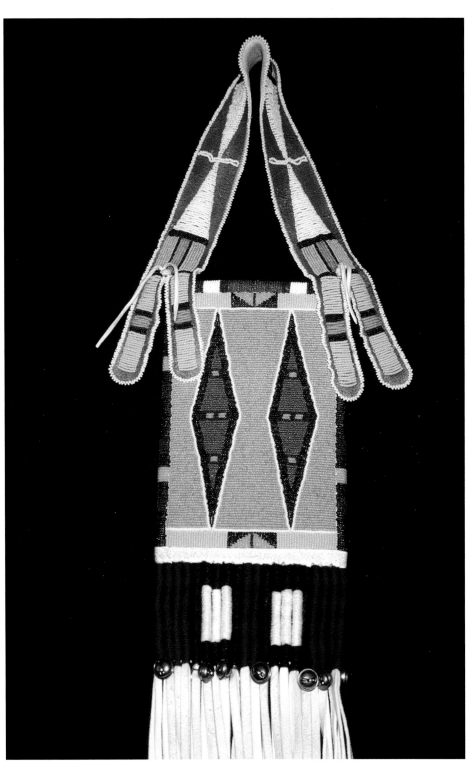

Mirror Bag. Crow-style design worked in Crow running stitch. Tim Monaghan, 2000. Collection of the artist.

Detail, Bag.

Personal Bag of Charles Eagle Plume.
An unusual combination of styles and
materials. The lower portion is sinew-
sewn lane stitch in typical Sioux style.
The upper portion is worked in
embossed stitch with very fine faceted
beads. Stems are sewn down one bead
at a time in a herringbone pattern. The
floral motifs are more typical of the
Santee or Eastern Lakota.
Charles Eagle Plume collection.

LOOM BEADWORK

Belts. Pan-Indian-style
tension loom work.
David Dean, 1979.
Collection of the artist.

Loom beadwork is somewhat uncommon among early Native American work, although it was practiced among the eastern, Great Lakes, and Midwest tribes. As modern powwow dancing developed, many more tribes began to use this technique. Today, loom beadwork is the most common technique used in Oklahoma to create fancy dance clothes, dance belts, and other large flat pieces of work.

TENSION LOOMS

Before the arrival of Europeans, Native American loom work originated with a tension loom designed to weave porcupine quills. The loom was almost identical to a small bow loom. Once beads became available, beadwork produced on a loom—either a two-bar or bow loom—was the next natural progression. Early pieces of loom beadwork were not large, usually measuring less than two inches wide and fourteen inches long.

Tension looms became larger as Europeans, often Jesuit priests sent to "civilize" the Native population, introduced looms designed to weave cloth. Europeans had already adapted these cloth looms for weaving beads, and Natives increased the size of their looms as they came to understand how versatile the larger looms could be.

▪ Two-bar looms

The two-bar loom consisted of warp threads anchored to a stiff piece of leather on both ends. The holes in the leather were made with an awl and the thread was passed through the holes. The leather served as the spacer bars for the loom. The warp thread continued through the spacers. One end was tied to a tipi pole or the weaver's foot; the other end was tied to the weaver's belt. By moving back from the weaving, the weaver adjusted the tension on the warp threads. This construction is probably the very earliest and simplest type of tension loom.

▪ Bow looms

The next variation of the tension loom was the bow loom. The warp threads were sewn through holes in a stiff piece of leather or wrapped around a small spacer stick. The leather or spacer stick was then tied to one end of the bow loom. The warp ends were attached to a length of green tree branch that, being longer than the warp threads, was made to bow. The threads were held under tension as the limb tried to return to its original unbowed state. Small tension looms of this type are easy to make and simple to operate.

▪ Box looms

The next development in Native loom

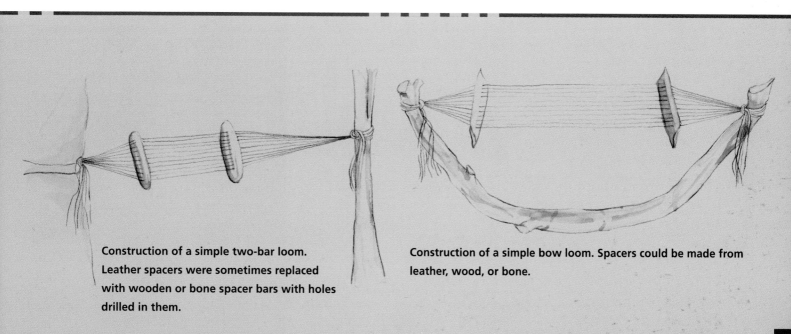

Construction of a simple two-bar loom. Leather spacers were sometimes replaced with wooden or bone spacer bars with holes drilled in them.

Construction of a simple bow loom. Spacers could be made from leather, wood, or bone.

BUILDING A BOX LOOM

A simple box loom can be created from scrap lumber.

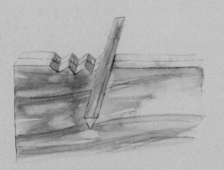

Clap the header boards together before constructing the box and file grooves in both pieces at the same time.

design was the box loom. Box looms made it possible to create wider pieces of beadwork. As the name implies, the shape and design of the loom resembled a box, and the frame could be made from almost any wood, in almost any dimensions. Box looms were common among the Midwest tribes where they were used to build large bandoleer bags in the early 1870s. The advantage of this type of loom is that it takes up a relatively small space while it allows the creation of large pieces of beadwork.

The first box looms were probably made from fruit shipping crates, and box looms can, in fact, be created from almost any scrap lumber. To make the header boards that hold the warp threads in place, file separation grooves in the boards with a small triangle file. To insure that you have equal distances between the spaces in both header boards, clamp the boards together in a vise and file the grooves in both pieces at the same time. You can also connect springs across the ends of the header boards to make spacers.

HOW TO BUILD A TENSION LOOM

There are as many different tension loom designs as there are beadworkers to work on them. Here is a simple yet serviceable tension loom that anyone can build. As you do more and more loom work, you will undoubtedly design different looms to suit your purposes. Looms that are six to eight inches wide and twenty-two to thirty inches long will be large enough for most pieces you'll want to bead.

■ Materials

1" × 8" lumber, three feet

1" × 2" lumber (for braces), one foot

two ¼" diameter door springs (slightly shorter than the width of the loom)

14 wood screws

2 or 4 screws to hold the warp (depending on the width of the loom)

First cut the 1" × 8" wood to the dimensions that will suit your needs. Cut triangles of an appropriate size from the 1" × 2" lumber for braces. The braces are important because when the loom is warped, a lot of strain is put on the header boards—the braces give the header boards additional strength. Screw the spring spacer rods to the top of the header boards. Attach the screws that will hold the warp to the outside of the header boards. Sand all pieces of wood so there are no rough spots to snag clothing or furniture. It is also not a bad idea to put cork or felt feet on your loom to protect tabletops. You may consider gluing a ruler to the baseboard as a means of keeping up with the length of your work as it progresses.

WARPING A TENSION LOOM

Possibly the best thread for loom work is polyester; it is very strong with little stretch. To warp the loom, start by tying the thread to one of the screws on the end of the header board. Pull the thread over the header board and through the middle of the spacer spring. Bring the thread over to the other header board and through the spacer spring opposite the warp end. Go around the screw in the header board and go back to the other header board, placing the warp in a spacer spring slot immediately next to the first thread. Continue to thread the loom in this manner, working away from the center on both sides, until the number of spaces between the threads equals the number of beads in the width of your design; you will need one more thread than the number of beads. If you want a design with a center row, you will need an odd number of spaces, which require an even number of threads. It is a good practice to double the outside threads to give your finished piece additional strength.

BEADING ON A TENSION LOOM

Once the loom is warped, thread a needle with a single thread that is a comfortable length to work with. Tie the thread to one of the outside warp threads with a simple overhand knot. It is good to leave a long tail so that the bead spacing can be adjusted in the first row. You will seldom find beads that match the spacing in your header boards exactly. It is better to have a little too much spacing so that the beads can be pulled and tied off properly. (If your beads are much too large for the spaces in the header boards, you can warp the loom with two spaces between each warp thread.)

BUILDING A TENSION LOOM

A simple tension loom can be made to the appropriate size for almost any project.

A spring screwed to the header board makes a simple spacer for holding warp threads.

Warps run parallel from one end of the loom to the other.

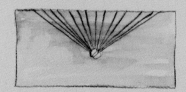

Warp ends are anchored to a screw at each end of the loom.

BEADING ON A TENSION LOOM

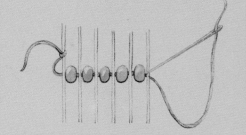

Stretch the beads *under* the warps and push them up so there is one bead between each set of warp threads.

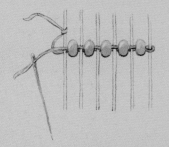

Thread the needle back through the beads, making sure the thread passes *over* the warp threads.

Once the weft thread is tied to the warp, thread the number and color of beads that match the first row of your bead pattern. Stretch the beads across and *under* all the warp threads and push them up through the spaces between the warp threads, one bead in each space. Once all beads are in their proper position, pass the needle back through the beads and *over* the warp threads.

HEDDLE LOOMS

As previously mentioned, loom beadwork was not the most common technique among early Native American tribes. And although some Natives practiced tension loom beadwork, it was historically not the most common kind of loom beadwork; many beadworkers today consider it the "standard" loom technique, but this was not always the case. The reason for the misconception stems from work done during the 1940s and 1950s by two gentlemen named Ben Hunt and Buck Burshears. They were involved with youth groups like the Boy Scouts, YMCA, and Campfire Girls. Loom beadwork was part of their camp program for young people, and they felt it was imperative to teach a technique that was easily understandable. Hunt and Burshears were widely published, and because generations of young people attended their camps across the country and learned the tension loom technique, it became known as the Native standard.

While Ben Hunt and Buck Burshears were teaching tension loom beadwork, John

Lotter was working just as hard to keep alive heddle loom work, a technique that was more widely practiced by Native people. John worked for years around the Chicago area and close to the Ho Chuck reservation in Wisconsin, teaching heddle loom techniques to Scouts and other persons interested in learning Native techniques. Heddle loom beadwork involves the use of a rigid heddle or guide that is threaded on the warp threads and used to separate them into two groups so that beads can be positioned between the groups. This is the same setup that is used to weave cloth. Double warped, heddle loom work is the strongest beadwork that can be done because so much thread is woven into a piece. Although I have found no museum examples of heddle looms, there are many museum examples of Native crafted heddles. Most are hand carved from walnut or some other type of hardwood.

HOW TO BUILD A HEDDLE LOOM

For heddle loom beadwork you need a heddle, a loom, and a shed rod. The important thing to keep in mind when you're designing a loom that will be used with a heddle is that there needs to be some way to adjust the tension on the warp threads as the work is being done. With the loom described here, the tension is adjusted by loosening the wing nuts that hold the rods to which the warp threads are attached, rotating the rods for tighter or looser tension, and tightening the wing nuts.

Materials

1 piece of ½" cabinet plywood, 8" × 26"

five ¼" wing nuts

one ½" diameter spring (slightly shorter than the width of the loom)

six #6 or #8 self-threading sheet metal screws

two #6 or #8 wood screws, 1" long

five ¼" carriage bolts, 8" long

10 flat washers that fit the bolts

1 piece of ⅛" dowel rod the width of the loom

1 piece of ¾" heavy walled PVC pipe, 45" long

Assembly

1. Using the illustration as a guide, draw two C-shaped side rails on the plywood. The headers should be 1¼" wide and 4"–5" high; the rails should be 1½"wide and as long as the work you intend to do plus about 6" for heddle operation. Cut the rails with a hand or band saw, rounding the tops of the headers. Sand all edges and corners to a smooth finish.

2. Drill ¼" holes in both side rails for the bolts to pass through, one at the top of one header end and four along the rails. (See illustration.) Drill two ⅟₁₆" pilot holes on the other header where the spring separator will be screwed into place.

BUILDING A HEDDLE LOOM

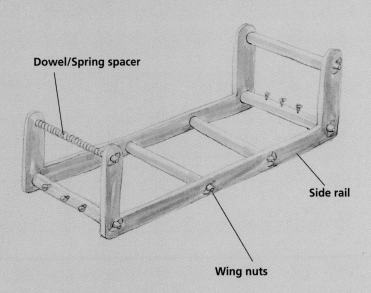

Dowel/Spring spacer

Side rail

Wing nuts

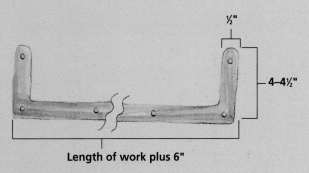

½"

4–4½"

Length of work plus 6"

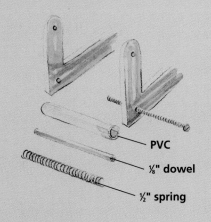

PVC

⅛" dowel

½" spring

3. Temporarily insert the 8" carriage bolts into the loom and measure the inside distance between the rails; this is how long the PVC pipe will need to be cut.

4. Using a hacksaw, cut five pieces of PVC pipe to the measurement determined in Step 3. The two pieces of PVC at the outer bottom edges will hold the threads as the loom is warped. Drill three ⅛" pilot holes evenly spaced along these two pieces of pipe. Screw in the self-threading metal screws to the point that their tips can be seen on the inside of the pipe.

5. Make a thread separator rod with the spring and the wooden dowel. Stretch the spring slightly to the measurement determined in Step 3; stretching will add a little more space between each spring curl. Using a hand or band saw, cut the dowel to the measurement determined in Step 3. Insert the dowel inside the spring. Screw the dowel to the side rails with the wood screws.

6. Thread the carriage bolts through one of the side rails, through a piece of PVC pipe, then through the other side rail. Fasten with a washer and a wing nut.

▪ The heddle

The heddle is a thin piece of wood with a series of slots and holes placed close together. When the heddle is strung on the loom, it separates the warp threads to create a shed so that beads can be placed between the warp threads. Native heddles had bird and animal figures carved into the top, resembling those brought to this country by Scandinavian immigrants. This feature is consistent with the fact that heddle beadwork was done by tribes of the upper

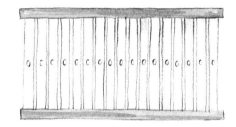

Midwest, an area heavily settled by Scandinavian immigrants.

Making a heddle is a tricky job, but with patience you will succeed. Make a heddle as wide as the widest piece of work you expect to bead, usually from 5" to 6". A twenty-five to fifty bead heddle should be sufficient. The heddle should be 3½" to 4" deep.

▪ Materials

⅛" hardwood such as maple, walnut, ash

¼" hardwood for end boards

wood glue

Cut heddle wood into ⅛" wide strips of the desired length. The number of strips you need depends on how many beads you want your heddle to handle. Measure to the center of each strip and drill a hole.

Set up a jig with two ¼" end boards, cut to appropriate width. Using wire finishing nails as spacers, glue the ends of each strip to the end boards and space the strips ³⁄₃₂" apart. When the glue has dried, glue another end board to the other sides of the strips.

▪ The shed stick

A shed is the space between warp threads that has been created by raising or lowering the heddle. The shed stick is used to keep the shed open while a string of beads or a weft is inserted. The shed stick should be a couple of inches longer than the widest work you expect to do. Make a shed stick from a 1" to 1½" dowel. Form a blunt point on each end by carving the stick with a sharp knife and sanding all the rough spots. Sand the stick with very fine sandpaper to

Shed stick

avoid snagging the warp threads as you pull the stick in and out of the warp.

WARPING THE LOOM AND THE HEDDLE

Once they get the hang of how to use a heddle loom, most people say that it less time consuming than using a tension loom because you go through the beads only once; however, it will take at least twice as much time to warp the loom. On a heddle loom, each warp must be tied off before the next can be strung. Unlike a tension loom, only one end of the heddle loom has a thread separator rod.

To warp a heddle loom, measure a length of thread to go across the loom from end crossbar to end crossbar, plus enough to tie off with, then double this amount and cut the thread. Tie the center of the thread to the center screw on one end crossbar. Pull the doubled thread over the middle of the thread separator rod and position it in one of the spaces. Pull the doubled thread apart and thread one through the middle hole in the heddle. Put the other thread through the slot to the left or right of the hole that the first thread is strung through. Pull the threads to the other end of the loom and tie them to the middle screw in the end crossbar. To add another thread, repeat this procedure, always threading through a hole and a slot next to it in the heddle. If your second thread is threaded to the left of the center thread, the third thread should be threaded to the right of the center thread to keep things even. If you have trouble pushing the thread through the holes or slots, use a Big Eye needle as a heddle threader. Insert one end of the Big Eye needle through the slot or hole, insert the thread through the needle, and pull the needle through the heddle.

Thread the loom with enough tension so that the heddle will not sag. Once you have threaded enough warps to create the number of spaces needed for your pattern, you are ready to proceed with the beadwork.

WARPING THE LOOM AND HEDDLE

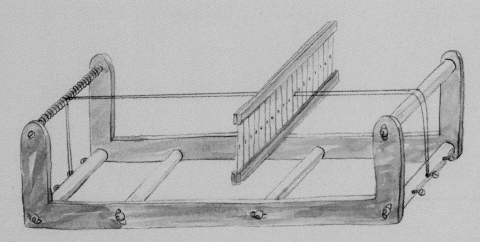

This heddle loom is shown with one round of warp thread.

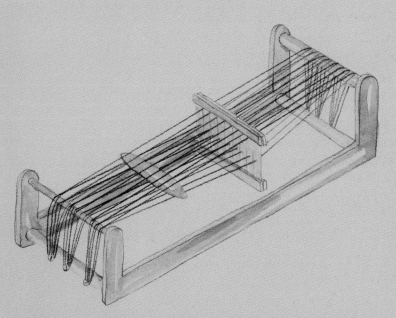

Warp threads are raised or lowered by means of the heddle, and the opening is held in place with the shed stick while a row of threaded beads is inserted.

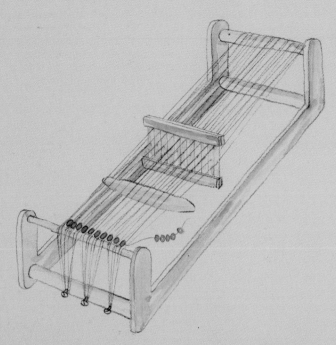

The shed stick holds the shed open so you can pass a weft of beads through.

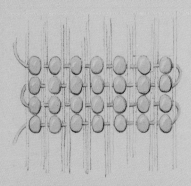

Heddle loom work can be identified by the edge thread, which passes from one row to the next instead of passing back through the same row of beads, and by the pairs of warp threads that pass alternately over and under each row of beads.

BEADING ON A HEDDLE LOOM

The first row of beadwork on a heddle loom is done the way the first row of beadwork is done on a tension loom. This first row sets up the proper spacing for all other rows. Just remember that there is a doubled thread between each bead as the first row is locked into place. For the second row, pull up on the heddle; when the threads are separated, insert the shed stick into the space between the warps. The shed stick's only purpose is to keep the shed open and allow you to work with both hands. String beads on the weft thread to match your pattern and insert the threaded beads through the shed. With a toothpick, bamboo skewer, old dental tool, or just about any instrument with a small sharp end, move the beads into their proper position—one bead in each space with a thread on each side of the bead. Once you've done this, remove the shed stick, push the heddle down, and insert the shed stick into the new space. You are now set up for the next row.

If you are working on a really wide piece of beadwork, stick the needle into a pencil eraser, then use the pencil to pull the thread through the shed. Never use the heddle as a tool to "pack" the rows of beadwork—it is too fragile to stand up to the pressure of packing.

Sash. Southern Plains, c. 1900. Tension loom work. Charles Eagle Plume collection.

When we go hunting it is not our arrow that kills the moose, however powerful be the bow; it is nature that kills him.

Big Thunder, Wabanaki Algonquin

Woven Band. Tension
loom work. Charles
Eagle Plume collection.

Peace. . .comes within the souls of men when they
realize their relationship, their oneness, with the
universe and all its powers and when they realize
that at the center of the universe dwells Wakan
Tanka, and that this center is really everywhere,
it is within each of us.

Black Elk, Oglala Sioux 1903

COMMON LOOM TECHNIQUES

Most loom work techniques are the same
for both the tension and the heddle loom.
A heddle loom is essentially a tension loom
that uses a heddle to manipulate the warp
threads.

▪ Adding a new weft thread

To add a new weft thread, begin by threading your needle with the new thread. Tie a
small knot and pass the needle and thread
through the previous row of beadwork,
ending in position to start the new row, and
then continue the work. The knot will stop
inside a bead and anchor the thread.

▪ Finishing the beadwork

How you finish a piece of loom beadwork
is determined by its final use. If the piece
is to be backed with a backing material, finish the ends by placing masking tape over
the warp threads; when you sew the piece
to the backing material, tuck the ends under
the beadwork. If the piece is going to be
used without a backing, one way to end the
work is to weave a weft thread back and
forth through the warp threads, without
beads, for about ¼". Cover this section with
white craft glue and allow it to dry. The
warp threads can also be woven back into
the beadwork. While this is much more
time-consuming, it is the cleanest and probably the most secure method of finishing a
work.

LOOM STITCH DESIGNS

Designs for loom beadwork run the gamut from very simple to very complex. Possibly the most difficult thing to teach about designing Native style beadwork is color combination. Unlike contemporary beadwork, Native work makes use of the differences between colors rather than the way colors work in combination with each other. It is not uncommon to find colors that we may think work against each other used in the same piece of work, such as red, orange, yellow, and purple.

While there does exist a Midwest style that was common with the prairie tribes of the upper Missouri River area, most loom work found today will be of a more contemporary Pan-Indian design. Prairie designs typically followed abstract floral or Persian rug designs found in many homes of the period from 1875 to 1920. Pan-Indian designs follow large star designs, X designs, feather patterns, and Peyote church designs. The Pan-Indian style is the result of the coming together of many Native cultures in the modern powwow circle. Now it is no longer always possible to tell what tribe a design came from. Today, a design more commonly identifies a region of the country than it does tribal history.

Over the last fifty years a style that can be best identified as the Oklahoma style has developed. These designs have large, bold geometric motifs made complex by

Sash. Potawatomi, traded to the Kiowa war chief Onka. Wide heddle loom work with appliqué stitch rosette worked on buckskin. Charles Eagle Plume collection.

Leg Bands. Mesquakie-style design, worked on a heddle loom. Wayne Wagner. Private collection.

Shoulder Bag. Winnebago, c. 1880. Worked on a wide heddle loom with small beads. Trimmed with loom-beaded tabs and lane-stitch borders. Charles Eagle Plume collection.

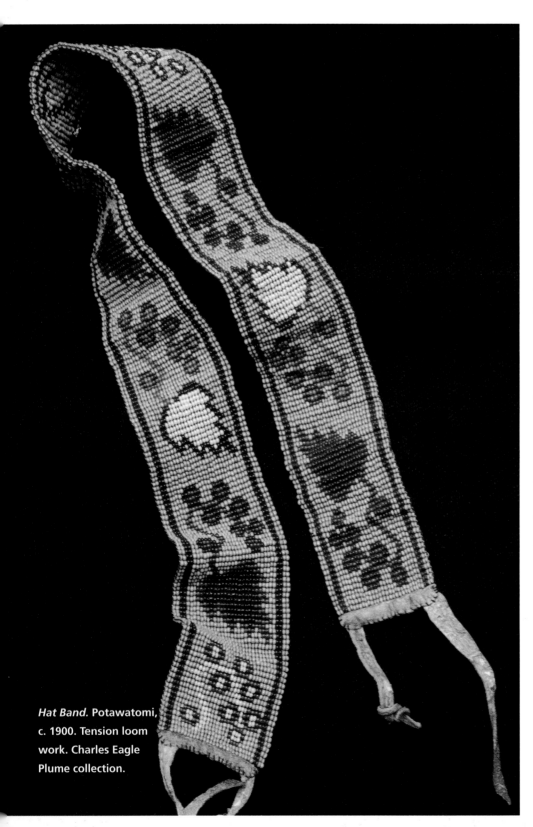

Hat Band. Potawatomi, c. 1900. Tension loom work. Charles Eagle Plume collection.

the addition of small details. Classic Oklahoma designs use very specific color combinations, often in a certain color spectrum such as red or blue. In one given piece there may be as many as six or eight different shades of a color. These designs are found on belts, fancy dance suspenders, and other large pieces of flat beadwork. While floral patterns do exist, they are found mainly in older prairie tribe designs.

Most Oklahoma work consists of geometric designs, most often with a center row, which means that there is an uneven number of beads in each row. Most patterns originate from this center row. Design elements in the Oklahoma style include eagle feathers, water birds, stars, American flag motifs, and other designs that can be used in combination with traditional geometric designs which go back to the older block designs found in lanestitch beadwork.

Most Native designed loom work will be less than sixty-five beads wide unless it is used for a bandoleer bag, which may be over one hundred beads wide. While almost any beads can be used for loom work, the most common are size 12° Czech beads. The simplest way to design a piece of loom beadwork is to start with graph paper and colored markers. Each square on the graph equals one bead. There are a number of computer beadwork design programs that give the beadworker more time to design and produce work.

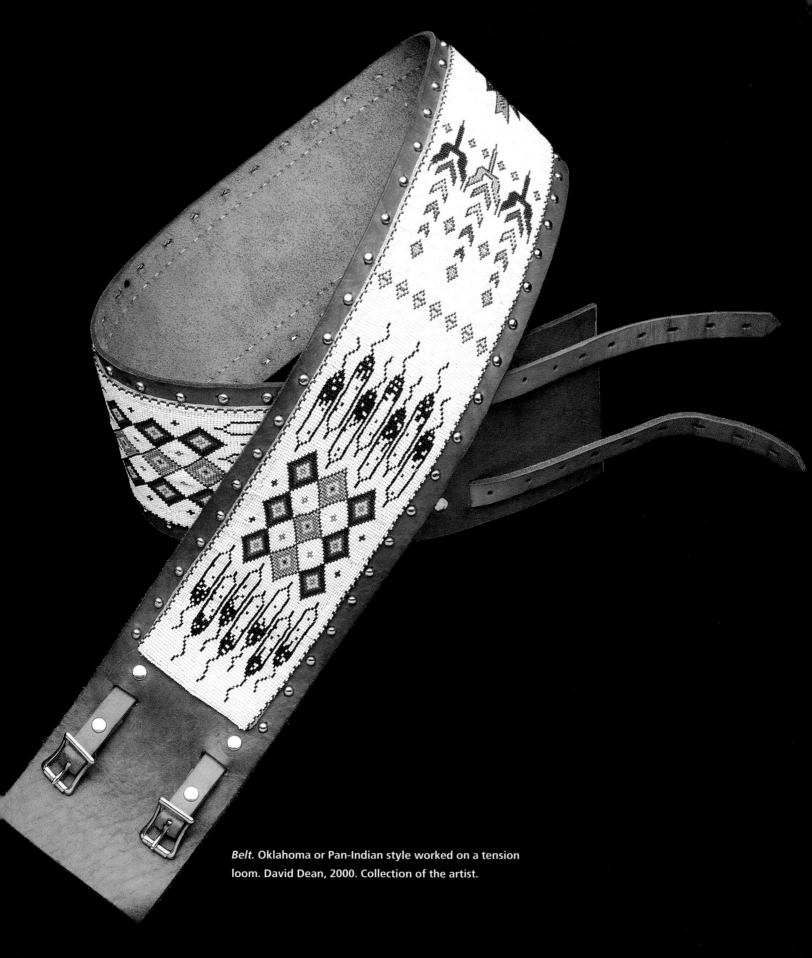

Belt. Oklahoma or Pan-Indian style worked on a tension loom. David Dean, 2000. Collection of the artist.

APPLIQUÉ BEADWORK

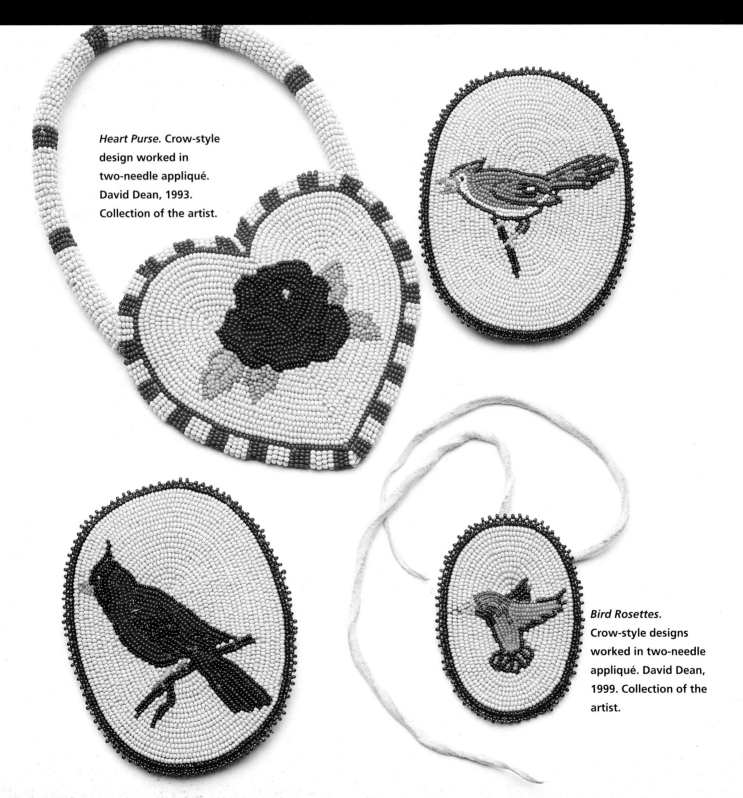

Heart Purse. Crow-style design worked in two-needle appliqué. David Dean, 1993. Collection of the artist.

Bird Rosettes. Crow-style designs worked in two-needle appliqué. David Dean, 1999. Collection of the artist.

With appliqué beadwork, a number of techniques can be used to achieve the same basic results. There are two schools of thought about how appliqué techniques developed. Some scholars believe the techniques were a natural outgrowth of quillwork methods used by Native people before the arrival of Europeans; many of the stitch techniques used in appliqué work are the same as those used in sewn quillwork. Appliqué techniques are also more often found in the work of tribes that had earlier produced extensive sewn quillwork.

Tribes such as the Crow, Blackfoot, Nez Percé, and Yakima produced a lot of appliqué beadwork, and their older form of art decoration was quillwork. The second school of thought suggests that appliqué techniques were taught to Native women in missionary schools and trading posts. Many of the stitches used in European embroidery are the same as those used in appliqué beadwork. In his monograph entitled "An Essay On Beadwork" (published on the Center for Bead Research website), Jamey D. Allen suggests that Native people were not just trading beads, but were also giving some instruction on what to do with them. This theory takes a very practical position—that European methods were added to the skills that Native women already had in working with quills and other natural products—and makes for a very logical conclusion. For myself, I believe that the development of all beadwork techniques was a combination of factors coming together at specific points in history.

The market influenced the style of beadwork that was produced. The trader

Belt Bag. **Crow-style design worked in two-needle appliqué. Don Drefke. Private collection.**

Bag. **Mesquakie-style design worked in two-needle appliqué. Wayne Wagner. Collection of the artist.**

who knew how to market his product could influence Native women to use skills they already possessed to create a new style of decoration. No matter what the exact history of appliqué beadwork, it is first of all extremely widespread, seen almost as much as lane-stitch beadwork. Second, it is an easily learned technique that yields quick results. Third, it is one of the most versatile beadwork techniques, one that allows the artist full expression with no limiting factors.

Designs used by the tribes that practiced appliqué techniques, including the Crow, Nez Percé, Blackfoot, Mesquakie, Iowa, Miami, and other tribes across the country, ran the gamut from geometric to abstract floral to realistic floral to human and animal forms. The only limiting factor was the beadworker's imagination.

Historically, appliqué consisted of beads sewn to brain-tanned buckskin or wool, and later canvas and other backings. To appliqué on buckskin, it is important that the stretch be pulled from the skin. This was accomplished by dampening a smoked hide and pulling the hide in every direction until it was dry. Not only did stretching the hide make it less likely to pull the beadwork sewn to it, stretching also made the buckskin bigger. Hides used for appliqué beadwork were not tanned as soft as possible because appliqué looks best on a slightly stiff hide. In many older pieces, whether buckskin or wool, a stiffening material, often brown wrapping paper, was used in conjunction with the backing material.

TWO-NEEDLE APPLIQUÉ

Two-needle appliqué beadwork, also called bead embroidery, is essentially a style of embroidery known as couching. The technique is also used in sewn quillwork, though most scholars believe that couching was probably taught to Native people by traders and missionaries in mission schools. Two-needle appliqué is probably a combination of techniques already known to Natives and those taught by Europeans.

Two-needle appliqué is possibly the most versatile type of beadwork that can be produced. The basic philosophy with this style of work is that if the design can be drawn it can be beaded. The only limiting factor to the detail that can be achieved is the size of bead used. It is common on very finely detailed pieces to find beads of a number of different sizes. Two-needle appliqué has been used in abstract floral, realistic floral, animal, human, and geometric designs. In older pieces, it is common to find appliquéd sections beaded separately and then sewn into position when the overall piece was finished.

The backing material used for two-needle appliqué ranges from fine woolens to leather to canvas to felt and even, historically, birch bark. With many of the older Native pieces, the backing material was used in combination with a stiffening material, often brown wrapping paper or bags. The backing materials were held taut in embroidery hoops while the work was being done. The stiffer the backing

materials, the better the beads stand up in the outlining rows. One of the best modern materials to use for backing is mending fabric (such as iron-on blue jeans patches), which can be purchased at most fabric stores. Cut two pieces of mending fabric a little larger than the completed project. Use a hot iron to fuse one piece of fabric to a sheet of typing paper (mending fabric holds a heat-activated glue). Once the first piece is in place, iron the second piece of fabric to the other side of the paper. This stiff "sandwich" can be used as backing material for beadwork done without the aid of an embroidery hoop. You can change the stiffness of the material by changing the thickness of paper ironed between the pieces of fabric.

You can make another type of backing from a cotton flannel baby bedsheet. Mix one part white glue and three parts water. Completely saturate the sheet with this mixture and hang it on a line to dry. Once dry, this backing is also stiff enough for beadwork done without the aid of an embroidery hoop.

After preparing the backing material, you should draw your design on the fabric. You need not be a great artist; many designs can be found in children's coloring books, cross-stitch pattern books, leatherwork books, and other sources of simple line designs. Unlike some contemporary work, color shading on traditional Native pieces is not complex. The beauty of traditional Native work lies in the fine execution of simple designs.

As the stitch name indicates, it takes two needles to do this work. Threads can range from sinew to Nymo. One needle should be a short or sharp needle and the other a long loom beading needle. Using two different needles helps keep your thread in order as you do the work. Sew through a design line with the first (loom) needle from back to front. String the number of beads necessary to reach from this first design line to a place that intersects another design line. Pull the thread so that the first two beads are tight against the backing material. Bring the second needle through the backing material and make a stitch over the first thread, up against the second bead. Continue in this manner, taking a couching stitch after every two beads. Do not skip more than two beads without taking a stitch; if you skip three or more beads the strung beads will bow slightly and give the finished piece an uneven appearance. It is also important not to crowd the beads; otherwise the work will cup instead of lying flat. When you use a cupped piece, it will gradually fall apart due to the stress put on the threads. However, it is okay to have small spaces in your appliqué that are not filled with beads—the human eye makes an adjustment and sees the spaces as filled.

Sharp points in a design are made by sewing the bead at the end of the point through the material—if the point is stitched with the usual couching method, the point will be more rounded.

TWO-NEEDLE APPLIQUÉ

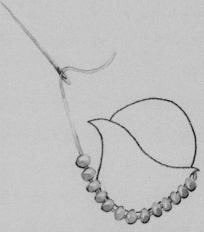

String enough beads to complete an entire design line.

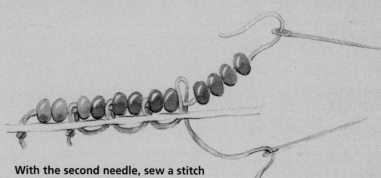

With the second needle, sew a stitch over the thread from the first needle every two beads.

Cupping occurs when beads are crowded into place.

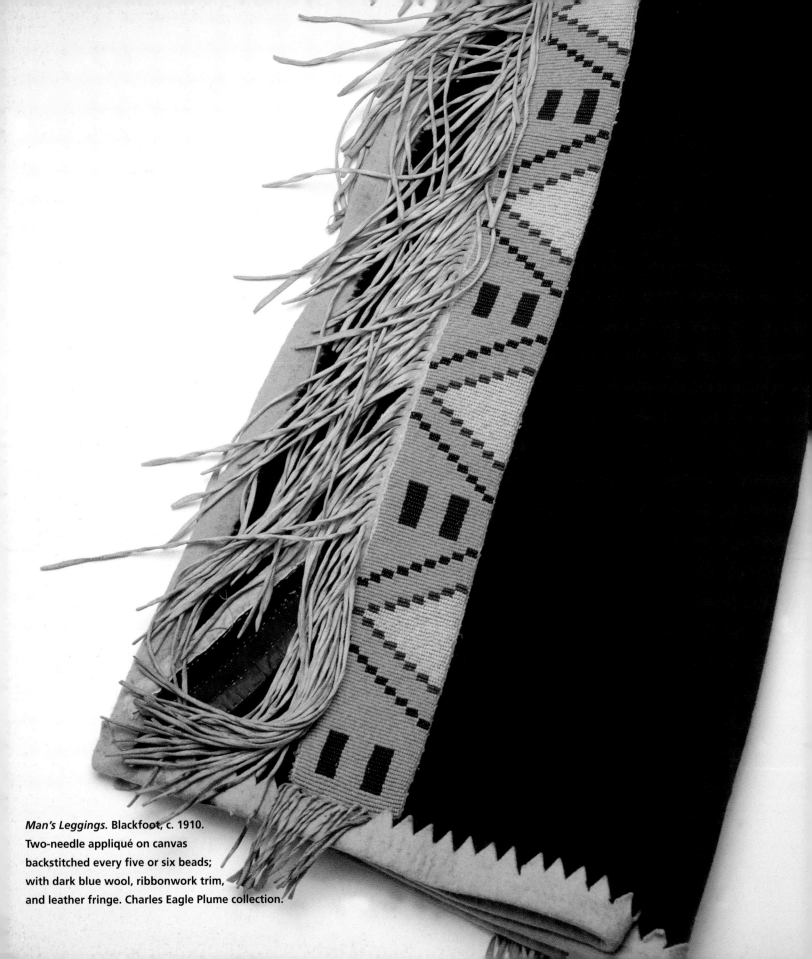

Man's Leggings. Blackfoot, c. 1910.
Two-needle appliqué on canvas
backstitched every five or six beads;
with dark blue wool, ribbonwork trim,
and leather fringe. Charles Eagle Plume collection.

Beadwork. Two-needle appliqué on canvas with red wool binding.
Provenance not known. Charles Eagle Plume collection.

Never be afraid to cut out work you've done that does not meet your
standards and replace it with the best that you can give the piece.

David Dean

CROW RUNNING STITCH

Wooden frame made from 1" × 2" pine.
Hide is tacked to frame using map tacks.
Design is drawn on hide.

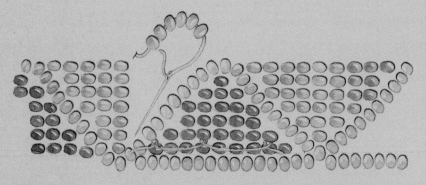

Design lines are done with two-needle appliqué, and the interior spaces are filled with Crow running stitch.

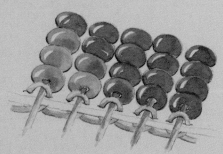

A row of backstitches is sewn across the design every two to five beads.

CROW RUNNING STITCH

The Crow, Nez Percé, Yakima, and other tribes that lived in the upper northwest plains of the country used Crow running stitch almost exclusively. This beadwork technique uses a combination of two-needle appliqué and running stitch. The designs were usually geometric, taken from painted designs on parflèches. While identification of many older pieces of beadwork may be questioned in terms of tribal origin, there is seldom a question about the origin of a piece of work produced by these tribes. They used bold color and striking geometric designs.

Generally, but not always, the outlines of Crow designs are first beaded in two-needle appliqué. The interior of the design is then beaded with the Crow running stitch. In some pieces, there seems to be no real rhyme or reason as to how designs are laid out or when two-needle appliqué or Crow running stitch is used; the beadworker used both techniques interchangeably. In addition, it is common to find the outside edges of a piece of Crow running stitch work done in single lane stitch.

To produce work in Crow running stitch, the buckskin or other backing material must be held taut in a frame of some sort. At left is an example of a simple wooden frame with the hide tacked to it and pulled taut.

Once the hide is stretched in a frame, draw the design with a pencil. Next, bead the design lines using the two-needle appliqué method (see page 64). Once you complete the outline of the design, insert the thread close to one of the design lines and string enough beads to go to the other side of the design. Insert the needle through the hide and bring it back up through the hide close to the design line. Add another row of beads, this time going to the other side of the design. Add rows in this way until a section is completely covered with rows of beads. Next, tack each row to the buckskin with lines of back stitching two to five beads apart. Thread a needle with a length of thread that is comfortable to work with and tie a knot at the end. Bring the thread through the hide from back to front between two beads just beyond the thread of the first row of beads in the section you want to tack down. Bring the thread back across the thread of the first row between two beads; insert the needle into the buckskin, and bring it back out just beyond the thread that connects the second row of beads. Repeat this process, passing under two rows and back over one. The more beads between the lines of back stitching, the looser the work will appear.

When done properly, this style of work has a bumpy appearance. The directions of the rows are totally up to the discretion of the beadworker, and row directions may change a number of times on the same piece of beadwork. By changing the direction of the rows, the work gains texture and develops a complex character. All types of beads were used in Crow running stitch and it is common to find different sizes of beads on the same piece. This feature also added to the character of the work. While buckskin is the best option for backing Crow running stitch, you can use canvas instead. If you use canvas, sew all stitches completely through the fabric.

"Flea" Bag. **Crow running stitch worked with sinew on buckskin with red wool binding. The work is very tight and fine. The lower edge is rolled. Charles Eagle Plume collection.**

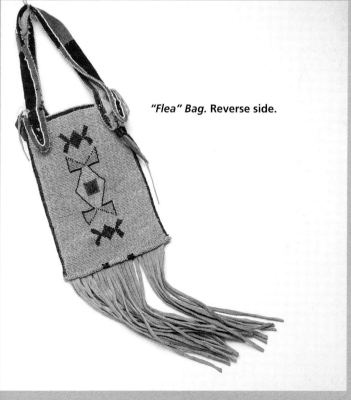

"Flea" Bag. **Reverse side.**

Bandolier Bag. Chippewa-style pattern worked in two-needle appliqué. Private collection.

Ceremonial Shirt. Crow, c. 1920. Crow running stitch and lane stitch with hair fringe. Charles Eagle Plume collection.

Vest. Two-needle appliqué on black wool. Charles Eagle Plume collection.

Back of Vest.

RETURN STITCH

Pull a threaded needle through the backing material from back to front. String two or three beads, pull them tight against the backing material along the design line, and push the needle back through the backing material. Bring the needle to the front again between the last two beads and pass the needle through the hole in the last bead.

The Great Spirit is in all things; he is in the air we breathe. The Great Spirit is our Father, but the earth is our mother. She nourishes us; that which we put into the ground she returns to us.

Big Thunder,
Wabanaki Algonquin

RETURN STITCH

Although return stitch is not a traditional Native American beadwork technique, I chose to include it because over the last fifty years it has been recognized as one of the best to use for beading rosettes and medallions, where exact bead placement is critical. Rosettes are round pieces of bead-work used to accent dance clothes. They are used on hundreds of items from bustles to dresses to neckpieces. Usually rosettes are beaded from the center and expanded outward. See page 79 for a full description of how to lay out a rosette.

The same backing materials and threads used in two-needle appliqué can be used with return stitch. Once you've prepared the backing material and drawn the design, pull a single threaded needle through the backing material from back to front on the design line. String two or three beads, pull them tight against the backing material along the design line, and push the needle back through the backing material. Bring the needle back to the front between the last two beads added and thread the needle through the hole in the last bead. Needle placement is critical when you're doing this stitch. The more precise you are with the needle the better the work will appear.

DESIGNS FOR APPLIQUÉ

Designs for appliqué techniques fall into a number of categories and are limited only by imagination. The following is a brief description of each category and the tribes that might have used them. Designs tend to be regional. For example, the people of the upper Midwest, including the Oto, Missouri, Potawatomi, and Mesquakie, used abstract floral designs almost exclusively in their beaded creations. It is thought that the people first saw these designs in French trade Persian rugs and paisley printed materials. Whatever the designs' origin, the color combinations used by Native beadworkers give the designs a definite flair. Periwinkle blue, emerald green, transparent red, and primary yellow may seem an odd combination, but it was commonly used by Oto and other upper Missouri River tribes.

Many abstract floral designs can be split in half or even quartered. Each half or quarter may be beaded in a different color. It is common to find the quarters diagonally across from each other beaded in the same color. The outlines of the designs are almost always beaded with a double row of white beads. Abstract floral designs were commonly worked on red, navy blue, or black wool cloth.

Designs used by the Crow, Nez Percé, Wasco, Yakima, and other Plateau tribes fall into two categories. The first includes transmountain or geometric style designs which are outstanding for their bold use of color. Many of these designs were probably first painted on parflèches.

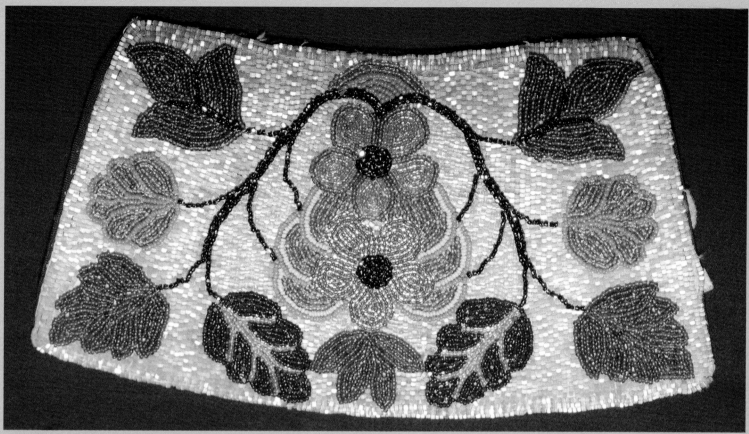

Cuff. Chippewa-style design worked in two-needle appliqué. Wayne Wagner. Private collection.

Arm Bands. Crow-style design worked in two-needle appliqué. Don Drefke. Collection of the artist.

Trapper's Jacket (details). Worked in small beads on fine, soft buckskin, these appliquéd motifs are padded with brown paper to give an embossed effect. Charles Eagle Plume collection.

Shoulder Bag. Ojibwa, c. 1870. Two-needle appliqué in large beads. Charles Eagle Plume collection.

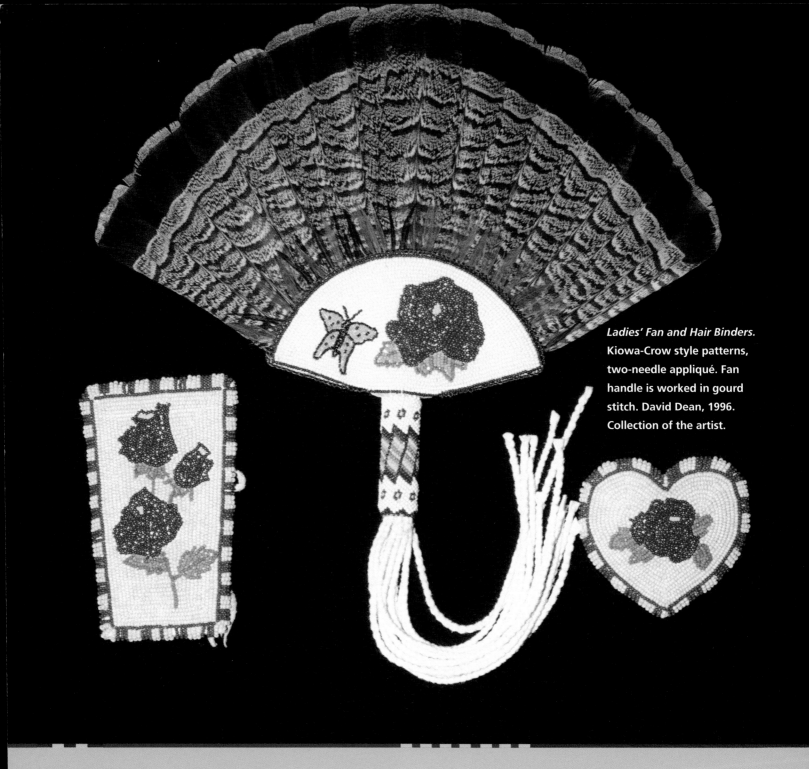

Ladies' Fan and Hair Binders.
Kiowa-Crow style patterns,
two-needle appliqué. Fan
handle is worked in gourd
stitch. David Dean, 1996.
Collection of the artist.

If men would seek what is best to do in order to make themselves worthy of that toward which they are so attracted, they might have dreams which would purify their lives. Let man decide upon his favorite animal and make a study of it, learning its innocent ways. Let him learn to understand its sounds and motions. The animals want to communicate with man.

Brave Bull, Teton Sioux

Picture Bag, Purse, and Hair Binder.
Crow-Nez Percé style patterns, two-needle appliqué.
David Dean, 1991. Collection of the artist.

The old Lakota was wise. He knew that man's heart away from
nature becomes hard; he knew that lack of respect for growing,
living things soon led to lack of respect for humans too. So he
kept his youth close to its softening influence.

Chief Luther Standing Bear 1886

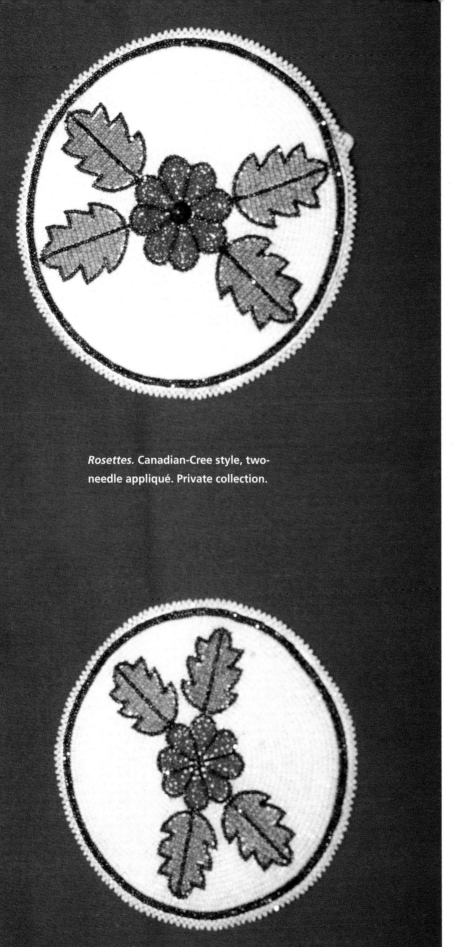

Rosettes. Canadian-Cree style, two-needle appliqué. Private collection.

The second category of designs used by the Crow, Nez Percé, Wasco, Yakima, and other Plateau tribes consists of realistic designs that depict the shapes of flowers, people, animals, birds, and other objects. Although some color shading was used in these designs, shading in traditional Native work was not as elaborate as it is in contemporary work.

The next design group includes the type used in creating rosettes or medallions. These patches of beadwork are mainly attributed to tribal people that live mostly in present day Oklahoma. Although the predominant style is geometric, some realistic designs are also seen.

BEADING THE ROSETTE

Rosettes are generally beaded with the return stitch. Begin at the center of the design and sew the center bead to the backing material. The first row will form a circle around the center bead. Sew this row using the return stitch, securing every other bead. Continue in this manner until you've beaded the entire design. Be sure to secure the last bead added.

Rosettes can also be stitched with two-needle appliqué. Begin at the center of the design and sew the center bead to the backing material. For the first row, string enough beads to form a circle around the center bead. Using the second needle, sew the row of beads in place every two beads.

Rosette Layout and Beading

Rosettes have an historical background as decoration for war bonnets, dresses, neckpieces, aprons, centers of bustles, bolo ties, and hundreds of other Native American goods. The techniques used to create rosettes include two-needle appliqué, return stitch, and lane stitch.

Designs used to bead rosettes include geometrics, realistic picture designs, and flowers. You can spend many hours designing rosettes. Here is the process for laying out the symmetrical geometric designs. You will need paper, pencils, a ruler, and a good compass.

Begin at the center of the design by sewing a single bead to the backing material. The first row will encircle this bead, and is worked in return stitch. Subsequent rows can be worked in two-needle appliqué.

1. With a ruler, draw a straight line 6" to 10" long on a piece of paper.

2. Place a compass on the line and draw a circle. The radius should be half the width of the desired final size of the rosette. Example: Set compass at 2" to create a 4" rosette.

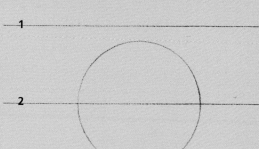

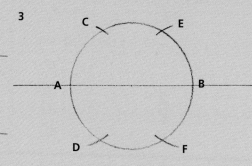

3. Keeping the compass on the same setting, go to point A and strike an arc on the circle at points C and D, then move the compass to point B and mark points on E and F.

4. With a ruler, carefully draw a straight line connecting points C and F and points D and E.

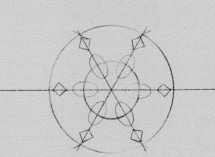

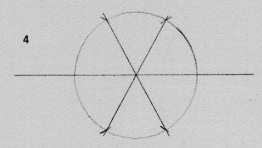

By using these radial lines and additional circles within the primary circle, you can produce rosette designs with a pencil, a ruler, and your imagination.

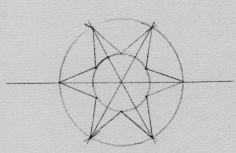

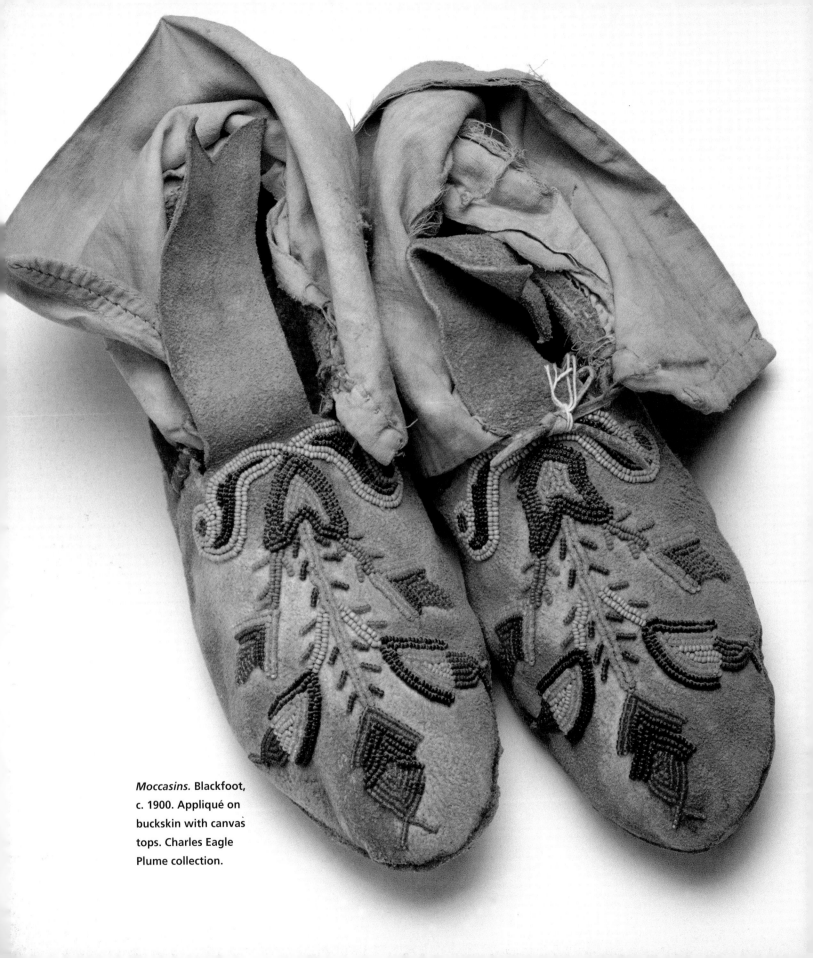

Moccasins. Blackfoot, c. 1900. Appliqué on buckskin with canvas tops. Charles Eagle Plume collection.

Octopus Bag. Tlingit, c. 1900. Different bead sizes and qualities have been used for the two-needle appliqué. Green silk ribbon and zipper stitch edgings trim the black wool bag. Charles Eagle Plume collection.

You are your toughest critic.

David Dean

GOURD STITCH AND COMANCHE BRICK STITCH

Feather Fan. Gourd stitch handle and
two-needle appliqué feather base.
David Dean, 1994. Collection of the artist.

Late in the timeline of Native American beadwork (between 1870 and 1890), the Kiowa and Comanche people of the southern plains began to use two beadwork techniques: gourd stitch and Comanche brick stitch. Europeans employed by the government as Indian agents and schoolteachers taught these techniques to Native people, and they became popular on the southern plains at the same time they were being used by Europeans to create beaded purses.

Once they learned the basic techniques, Native people developed a style that was distinct from its European counterpart. While most European work used designs of floral patterns and other dainty motifs for a market driven by women, Native people did their work in geometric forms, in color schemes that went totally against the accepted European use of color. European color schemes were very conservative; colors complemented each other and blended together. Native perception of color was totally different. Natives thought not of the color itself but of its intensity, viewing shades in terms of "hot," "cold," and "neutral." The Native beadworker did not pick shades that blended together but rather exhibited high contrast. Many designs used a series of colors that followed the traditional Native concept that colors should blend from dark to light. A spectrum was a common blend: red, orange, and yellow, followed by a dramatic contrast color such as blue.

In European circles, these techniques

Fan Handles. **Kiowa-style design, worked in gourd stitch. David Dean, 1994. Collection of the artist.**

were known as bead weaving, weaving on a bias, bias weave, diagonal weave without a loom, net weaving, and twill stitch. European beadworkers typically used these techniques to produce a fabric that formed a bag or other such object. In most Native circles, the name given to these stitches is gourd stitch or peyote stitch for one technique, and Comanche brick stitch or stacked stitch for the other. These stitches were used to cover objects such as cylindrical rattles, fan handles or gourds.

BEADWORK AND THE NATIVE AMERICAN CHURCH

It is important to understand the connection of gourd stitch and Comanche brick stitch with the Native American (peyote) Church. As these two techniques became prevalent on the southern plains, men began to produce the beadwork. This change was due to several factors. First, at this time most tribal people were relegated to reservations, a system under which many men found they had no way to spend time productively—until they saw that beadwork was a good way to add to the family's income. Second, women were not allowed to produce the accoutrements used in the peyote ceremony of the Native American Church, almost all of which are beaded; the handling of feathers and saying of prayers involved with the creation of Native American Church equipment were in men's domain. In many locations this philosophy is still in use today.

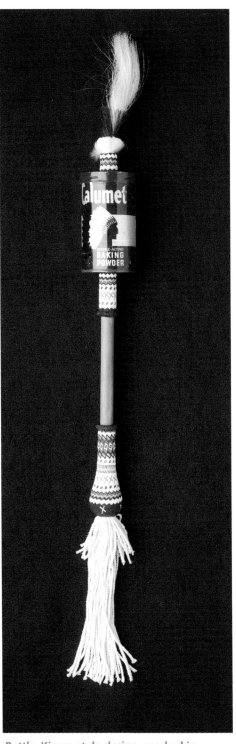

Rattle. Kiowa-style design, worked in gourd stitch. David Dean, 1994. Collection of the artist.

Before the introduction of gourd stitch and Comanche brick stitch, items used by Native people were usually beaded by wrapping beads around an object or, on occasion, attaching them to the buckskin covering. Use of the new techniques coincided with the development of the Native American Church which, in itself, became for the people relegated to the reservations a way to remain "Indian" and hold on to their traditions and culture. The peyote cactus is a sacrament in the Native American Church, and beadwork associated with church ritual items was said to be done in "peyote stitch." As such, the stitch is more than just a style of beadwork. Among Native people, peyote stitch is associated with a number of traditions, the major one being that it is used specifically to create items for use in the Native American Church, and appropriate prayers are always said as the work is created.

As peyote stitch grew in popularity, it began to make its way into the dance arena. In order to distinguish between work done specifically for the Native American Church and items used for dancing, a new term, "gourd stitch," was developed. Gourd dancing comes from the Kiowa Tiah-Pah Society, which is one of the original Kiowa war dance societies, and items beaded for gourd dancing are said to be done in gourd stitch. The stitch has no religious connotation and is therefore the "politically correct" term for this type of beadwork.

Again, the major difference between peyote stitched beadwork and gourd stitched beadwork is that an item beaded in peyote stitch has been made for religious purposes. How the work is done and what the final product looks like is essentially the same for both stitches. There are, however, some design elements that are used specifically for Church items, and they should be avoided when you are producing work for other purposes. Peyote flowers, crosses, and water bird designs are considered Church designs.

NATIVE ADAPTATION OF GOURD AND BRICK STITCH

As opposed to European purses and items made from flat fabric, almost all Native work done in both gourd and Comanche brick stitch is produced around a solid object such as a fan handle, drum stick, church staff, or gourd rattle. For this reason, Native people rewrote the rules concerning tension and how to use these stitches.

Native use of gourd stitch and Comanche brick stitch developed as the result of a combination of things: the "right" time in history, the will of the people to learn, the availability of materials and tools, and the ability of traders to market Native work. Threads and needles of European manufacture were critical to the development of the stitches. Sinew, awls, and bone needles are almost impossible to use in this kind of work, and much Native gourd-stitch and Comanche brick-stitch work held in museum collections is done with cotton or silk thread. Many of the finest

Dance Cane and Fan Handles. Kiowa-style designs, worked in gourd stitch. David Dean, c. 1980. Collection of the artist.

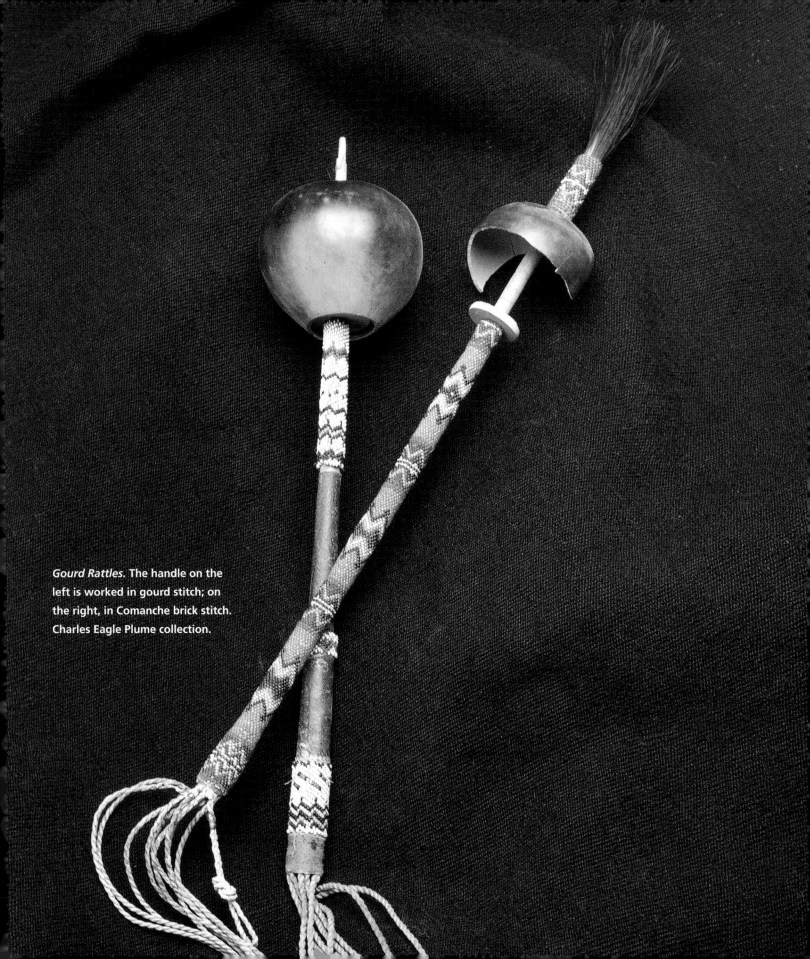

Gourd Rattles. The handle on the
left is worked in gourd stitch; on
the right, in Comanche brick stitch.
Charles Eagle Plume collection.

pieces of Native stitched work are produced in small beads, sizes 13° or smaller. Items used in the Native American Church are often beaded in 16° or 18° beads of Czech origin. Typically, Native works in large beads are made for the tourist trade and the very finest work is held back for family members. Typical fine items include fan handles, dance canes, gourd and shaker rattles (the latter are made from metal salt or pepper shakers and used in the gourd dance arena), side drops on leggings, bolo ties, dresses, and hair barrettes.

Around the late 1880s, many Comanche women began doing narrow bands of brick stitch on moccasins, one of the few instances of these stitches being used for flat work. (The fine items mentioned above have small round, solid tassels that were beaded in gourd stitch and brick stitch. Any flat work done on these items was usually done in lane stitch.) The Denver Art Museum has a brick-stitched cradle board beaded in size 9° beads, but this piece is the exception rather than the rule. Ninety-nine percent of the brick- and gourd-stitch work produced by the Native population is done around an object.

GOURD STITCH VERSUS COMANCHE BRICK STITCH

Both gourd stitch and Comanche brick stitch can be used for creating a net of beadwork, and through increasing and decreasing, the net takes the shape of the

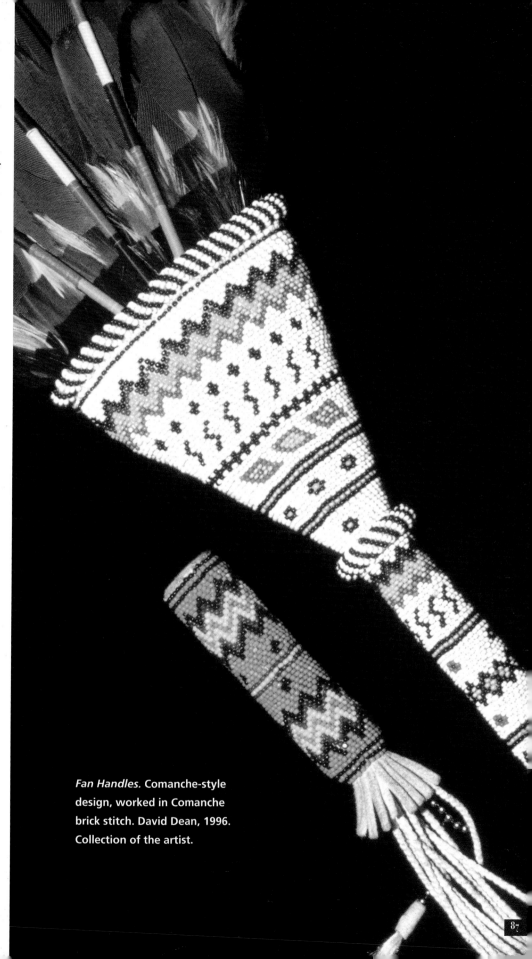

Fan Handles. **Comanche-style design, worked in Comanche brick stitch. David Dean, 1996. Collection of the artist.**

Gourd Rattles. **Detail of the photograph on page 86. Notice the different orientation of the beads in gourd stitch (left) and Comanche brick stitch (right). Charles Eagle Plume collection.**

object being beaded. However, gourd stitch was and is the more commonly used technique because it works up quickly. The major difference between the two stitches is the way the beads lie in relation to the object being beaded. In gourd stitch, the direction of the bead holes is perpendicular to the object; in Comanche brick stitch the beads stack up like bricks on a house. Another difference is in the way the work is produced. In gourd stitch the beads are woven together, and in Comanche brick stitch the threads are interlocked.

Brick stitch stayed almost exclusively with the Comanche tribe until about 1910 when a number of brick-stitched pieces began to show up in Osage circles. It is not clear whether these pieces were traded for or produced by Osage beadworkers. What is clear is that this is the time when the Native American Church began to spread from tribe to tribe and the Osage had a number of direct contacts with the Comanche tribe. Both peyote stitch and brick stitch beadwork are commonly used to decorate church items, and when used this way both are considered sacred.

HOW TO DO GOURD-STITCH BEADWORK

Two different styles of gourd-stitch beadwork were traditionally practiced by Native American beadworkers. One method is commonly referred to in contemporary circles as even-count gourd stitch. The other method, which is distinctive to Native beadwork, is called three-drop

gourd stitch. With both methods, symmetry of design is key.

■ Even-count gourd stitch

In order to maintain symmetry, many traditional Native American designs are based on a number of beads in a round that is divisible by six. However, any even number of beads will work with this technique, especially if you are beading simple stripes or spirals.

There are as many different ways to start gourd-stitch beadwork as there are people who do it. Once the work is started, it is all produced in the same manner. Here are two methods for starting gourd stitch. Either way is acceptable and will produce good work.

Starting even-count gourd stitch, method one

This is probably an old technique used to make gourd-stitch beadwork. First, cover the object that is to be beaded—a fan handle, for instance—with soft leather such as buckskin or goatskin. As the work progresses, the leather forms a "pocket" around each bead. These pockets protect the beadwork and prevent breakage in the event the object is dropped.

To cover an object with leather, first cut the leather a little larger than the object to be covered. Spread white glue on the leather and lay the object to be covered on top of the glue. Pull the leather tightly around the object and pinch the seam with a pair of pliers. The more you pinch the seam, the tighter the leather is pulled. Once the glue has dried, trim off the leather flush with the object. This technique works for covering a cylinder and odd shaped items such as fan handles.

I'll explain this start with a half-diamond design. Thread a needle with a length of thread that is comfortable to work with. This should be a single thread with a knot tied in the end. Pull the needle through a point on the buckskin at the top end of the object (I usually start at the seam). The first round of beads will be stitched to the buckskin. Because of the way the beads stack with even-count gourd stitch, each round consists of half the number of beads that will fit around the object, and for the first round they need to be sewn far enough apart that another bead can fit between each pair of beads.

The beads in the first (top) round are the color of the half-diamonds (dark). In this example, the first round consists of nine beads (the total number needed to encircle the object is eighteen). Space the beads as evenly as possible around the object. When the final bead of this round is in place, pass the needle through the first bead again to end the round.

For the second round, the pattern is two dark beads followed by one background (light) bead. Pick up a bead and pass through the next bead from the first round. Work this pattern of two dark beads and one light bead, passing through the next bead from the first round, to add nine beads total. When you reach the end of the

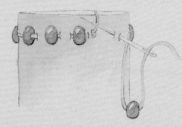

Space the beads evenly around, leaving room for one bead between each pair of beads. For the half-diamond design, the first row is made with red beads.

Pass the needle back through the first bead to end the round.

Begin the second round by picking up a bead and passing the needle through the next bead in the first row. Proceed all the way around.

The color sequence for the second round, according to the half-diamond illustration at the top of this page, is red-red-blue.

STARTING EVEN-COUNT GOURD STITCH, METHOD TWO

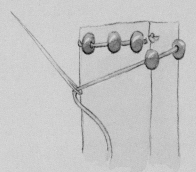

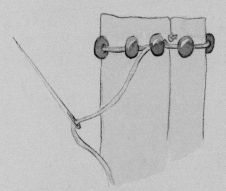

String half the number of beads needed to fill the diameter of the object. Wrap the thread around the object, and space the beads out evenly.

When you reach the end of the round, pass back through the first bead added in that round.

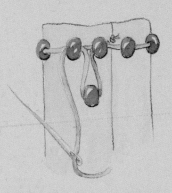

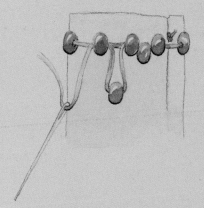

To begin the second round, pick up a bead and pass through the next bead.

Continue picking up a bead and passing through the next bead all the way around the object.

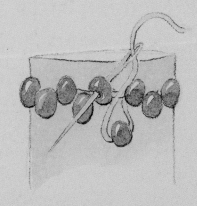

For the third round, pick up a bead, skip a bead, and pass through the next low bead.

round, pass back through the first bead added in that round.

For the next round, the color sequence is one dark bead followed by two light beads. As you work the third round, it will be obvious which beads to pass through. The beads added in the second round will hang down a little lower than the beads in the first round. Pick up a bead and pass through the next low bead. Repeat this process to the end of the round. Now do three or four rounds of background beads. Remember to end each round by going back through the first bead added in that round.

Starting even-count gourd stitch, method two

The second method is also worked over an object covered with soft leather. Start as for method one, pulling a threaded needle through the buckskin at the top end of the object at the seam. For the half-diamond design, string a number of dark beads to go completely around the object, adding or subtracting to end up with an even number that is divisible by six.

Take half the beads off the thread. Pass the needle through the first bead again. Pull the thread tight and space the beads evenly around the object. The color sequence and process for subsequent rounds is the same as for the first method. As with method one, finish each round by passing back through the first bead added in that round. It is critical that you do this; if you do not end each round by passing back through the first bead added, the design elements will be skewed and the finished product will look sloppy.

■ Three-drop gourd stitch

As Native people honed their skills in gourd-stitch beadwork, they developed a new style. Three-drop gourd stitch is a uniquely Native technique, and while at first glance it may look like even-count gourd stitch, close examination reveals that the beads stack differently. As the name indicates, the number of beads you begin with must be a multiple of three; in order to maintain symmetry of design, that number must also be even, or a multiple of six. Each round of beads added to the work consists of one-third the number needed to encircle the object. *Note:* If you are working with a design that does not call for symmetry, such as stripes or spirals, you may work with an odd multiple of three beads.

Starting three-drop gourd stitch

I'll explain this start using the modified half-diamond design (see below). String the number of dark beads needed to fit around your object and add or subtract until the number is divisible by six. Take off one third of the beads and space the re-maining beads evenly around the object. Pass through all the beads twice more, exiting from the first bead strung. These beads comprise rounds 1 and 2.

To form the third round, pick up a dark bead, skip a bead, and pass through the next bead. Repeat this process of picking up one dark bead, skipping one bead, and passing through the next bead all the way around the object. As you add each bead, be sure it stays below the beads of the round above. Finish the round by passing back through the first bead added. The beads should now form a slanted three-bead pattern.

To add subsequent rounds, string one bead and pass through the next lowest bead from the round above. Remember to end each round by passing back through the first bead added in that round.

The illustration below shows the color sequence to follow to get the modified half-diamond design. Note that to get this pattern, which has three beads stacked vertically, you must bead nine rounds. Because each round ends by passing back through the first bead added, the starting point for the subsequent round will move to the left; the starting bead for each round is outlined in bold on the chart.

After completing round 3, the beads will form a slanted three-bead pattern.

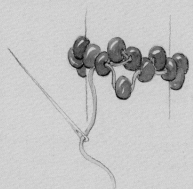

To add a round, string a bead and pass through the next lowest bead.

Beading sequence for the modified half-diamond design in three-drop gourd stitch. The starting bead for each round is outlined in bold.

■ Shaping the beadwork

Gourd-stitch beadwork can be used to cover objects of various shapes. One of the most common items beaded with this technique is a fan handle that has slope built into it, i.e., it is wider at some points than others. Increasing or decreasing gourd-stitch work can be a very time consuming and somewhat difficult process. Knowing when to increase or decrease seems to be the thing that plagues most beadworkers. I recommend that you increase or decrease at the sides of the object—most people look at fronts and backs, not sides.

Decreasing in gourd stitch

As your work progresses, watch very closely the edge of the previous round of beads. When the beadwork develops a slight ripple, it is time to work one less bead in the next round. When you decrease, you take beads out of the round, and therefore out of the scheme of the pattern. In order to keep designs symmetrical, beads must be dropped from the work in the background color. When a bead is taken out of the work, the diagonal that the bead would normally fall into is ended.

To decrease, simply go through the next bead of the work as you normally would, but do so without picking up a bead. On the next round, skip the place where the bead normally would have gone and place a bead through the next bead that is hanging down in the round. Look very carefully at the drawings below.

Increasing in gourd stitch

The space between each pair of beads should be equal to one bead. When the spacing begins to open up, it is time to add a bead to the round. As with decreasing, add beads in the background color to main-

DECREASING IN GOURD STITCH

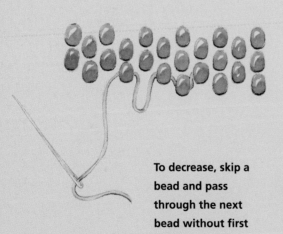

To decrease, skip a bead and pass through the next bead without first picking up a bead.

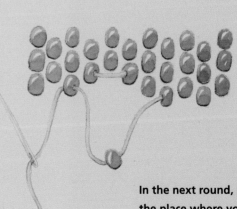

In the next round, pass by the place where you skipped a bead and go through the next low bead.

tain symmetry. When increasing, you are effectively adding an additional diagonal to the work. Once again, add beads only at the sides of the project. To increase, pick up two beads instead of one and proceed as usual. On the next round, sew into each of these two beads to create a new diagonal.

Perfecting decreasing and increasing

Decreasing or increasing creates a small triangle-shaped hole in the beadwork. This hole is caused by the interruption of the beadwork diagonal. To help hide the hole, use a felt tip marker to mark the leather the same color as the background. Remember also that the most effective place to decrease or increase is at the sides of the object and in the background color. Once the increase or decrease has been done and you are back to an area of the project that has no slope, it is important to drop or add enough beads so that you are back to a number that is divisible by six. In this way, you will maintain symmetry in your design.

▪ Gourd-stitch designs

When working with gourd-stitch beadwork designs, you must watch the diagonal as it develops. The diagonal is the key to reading designs and counting rounds. Diagonals will become prominent after the third round of beads is put into place. Gourd-stitch designs include a wide range of colors and symbols.

INCREASING IN GOURD STITCH

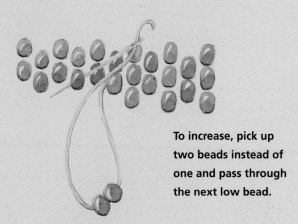

To increase, pick up two beads instead of one and pass through the next low bead.

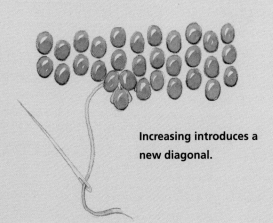

Increasing introduces a new diagonal.

Flat Fan. Kiowa-style design worked in gourd stitch. David Dean, 2000. Collection of the artist.

COMANCHE BRICK STITCH

Brick stitch came into use on the southern plains at the same time that gourd stitch was being developed in Native circles. Like gourd stitch, Comanche brick stitch is a woven net of beads that conforms to the shape of the object being beaded. The first major difference between the two stitches is that in brick stitch the beads stack vertically on the object, whereas in gourd stitch the bead holes are aligned horizontally. The second difference is that instead of the beads acting as the connecting system in the net, in brick stitch the threads are woven together. In brick stitch, the thread passes through each bead and loops over the thread between beads on the previous round to create a stacked effect like bricks on a house.

Starting Comanche brick stitch, method one

As with gourd stitch, there are many ways to start brick stitch, and just as with gourd stitch, the item should first be covered with soft leather (see page 88). The first way to start beading is to thread a needle with a single thread that is a comfortable length to work with. Knot the end of the thread. Sew the thread into a spot on the buckskin at the end of the object and at the seam. String two beads and take a small stitch into the buckskin. Go back through the last bead. String a bead and sew it to the buckskin so that it just touches the previously sewn bead. Once again, take a small stitch

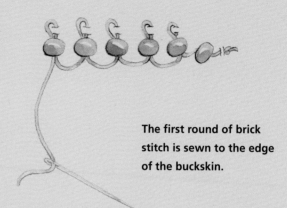

The first round of brick stitch is sewn to the edge of the buckskin.

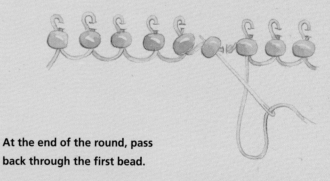

At the end of the round, pass back through the first bead.

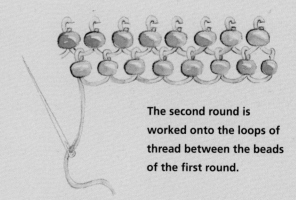

The second round is worked onto the loops of thread between the beads of the first round.

and pass back through the bead. Repeat this process until there is one round of beads all the way around the object. This first round should contain an even number of beads. When you approach the beginning of the round, pass through the first bead of the round.

To start the second round, string two beads and pass the needle up and over the loop of thread between the first and second beads of the first round. Pass back through the last bead added. Now pick up one bead and pass the needle up and over the loop of thread between the next two beads of the first round and pass back through the added bead. Repeat this process around the round. End the round by passing back through the first bead added in the round. As the beads begin to stack, it is very easy to see where each bead needs to be sewn.

▪ Starting Comanche brick stitch, method two

The second method for starting this stitch is to thread a needle, knot the end of the thread, and sew it into the leather as in the first method. Wrap the thread around the item. String two beads, pass the needle up and over the wrapped thread and pass back through the last bead. Next pick up one bead, pass the needle up and over the wrapped thread and back through the bead. Repeat this process, adding one bead at a time, until you reach the first bead that was sewn on the base thread. After adding the last bead, pass the needle through the first bead sewn to the base thread, loop around the thread, and pass back down through

---

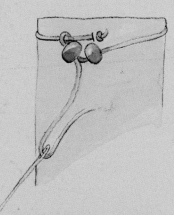

Start by stringing two beads and passing the needle over the wrapped thread and back through the last bead.

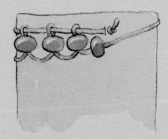

Add beads one at a time, passing over the wrapped thread and back through the bead.

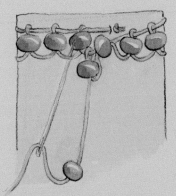

Add subsequent rounds by stringing a bead and passing over the loop of thread between two beads in the previous round and back through the bead.

the bead. This brings the thread down into position for the next round. Add subsequent rounds by stringing a bead, going over the loop of thread between two beads in the previous round, and back through the bead.

▪ Shaping the beadwork

As with gourd stitch, brick stitch can be increased or decreased to accommodate the shape of the object being beaded. As the work progresses, watch very carefully the edges of the previous rounds. When the beads become the least bit misaligned, it is time to either decrease or increase a bead.

▪ Comanche brick-stitch designs

Brick-stitch designs can be complex or simple, just like gourd-stitch designs. Many brick-stitch designs are the same as gourd-stitch designs, but visually converting the chart for the different method can be tricky—it's best to rechart the design on the proper grid. See appendix.

A bead artist can spend a lifetime perfecting gourd stitch and brick stitch. Only through trial and error with new designs and color combinations can one fully explore these techniques. Color becomes a design element all its own when you're producing these styles of beadwork. Rainbow color effects are common in Native-produced work. According to members of the Native American Church, many of the color rainbows produced in peyote stitch and brick stitch are inspired by the visions seen in church ceremonies.

DECREASING IN COMANCHE BRICK STITCH

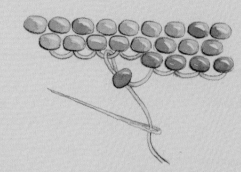

To delete a bead, simply skip a space where you would normally sew a bead.

INCREASING IN COMANCHE BRICK STITCH

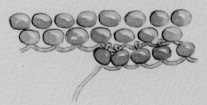

To add a bead, sew two beads into a space where you would normally add only one bead.

UNCOMMON BEADWORK TECHNIQUES

The first two techniques covered in this chapter developed and were practiced only in certain regions. They are very tribal specific and have limited distribution. Both techniques were derived from methods for other crafts. The third technique was adopted early and widespread among tribes.

EMBOSSED STITCH

Embossed or raised stitch is a technique practiced by Native people who resided in the upper northeastern part of the country, specifically the Iroquois, Seneca, Mohawk, and Canadian Cree tribes. Embossed stitch has its origins in the moose hair embroidery styles that these tribes used to decorate their goods. Moose hair embroidery and embossed beadwork techniques were used extensively to decorate dresses, moccasins and bags, ceremonial goods such as smoking hats, and other commonly used items.

Embossed beadwork usually uses large beads in the E bead to pony bead size. The work reached its pinnacle with the production of "whimsies," which have been sold at Niagara Falls since before 1880. For years, the Native people of the area have produced and sold embossed beadwork as a way to supplement their income, and whimsies have always been a popular product. These small pieces of beadwork are fashioned into change purses, pincushions, wall pockets, women's purses with both drawstring closures and metal-frame *Opposite: Arm Bands.* Winnebago-Menominee style worked in side stitch. Private collection.

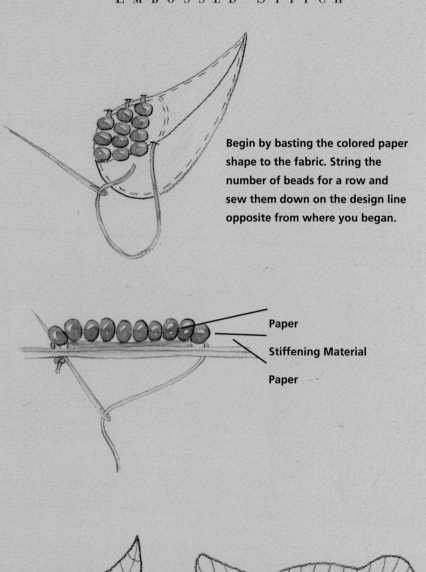

EMBOSSED STITCH

Begin by basting the colored paper shape to the fabric. String the number of beads for a row and sew them down on the design line opposite from where you began.

Paper

Stiffening Material

Paper

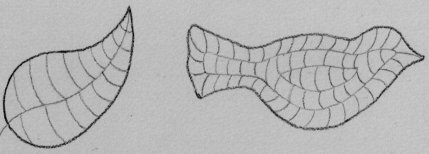

The bead rows may change direction to add a design element.

Purse. Seneca-Iroquois style,
c. 1880. Embossed stitch.
Collection of David Dean.

European closures, and other tourist-trade items. Many whimsies take the shape of a canoe, cowboy boot, or other common item; there are also traditional geometric shapes such as stars, triangles, and circles.

Embossed beadwork is typically done on fine cloth such as wool, silk, or taffeta. Sequins, silk ribbon, buttons, braids, and other sewing notions may be incorporated into the beaded pieces. The background fabric is usually stiffened on the back with a material such as brown paper grocery bags. In order to enhance the embossed effect, paper was also used under the beads on the front of the work. The embossed effect is achieved by using more beads in a row than what the design calls for. If the design calls for five beads in a row, six will be used so that they are crowded.

Translucent or transparent beads were commonly used for embossed beadwork, and the color of the resulting beadwork comes from the color of the filler paper used on the front side of the work, just under the beads. Clear beads pick up the color of the paper in a slight tint. In many older pieces, the colored paper of choice was Christmas wrap, in particular the foil type, and many varieties of bead shades were achieved. The edges of the work were often bound with a contrasting silk or taffeta ribbon, finished with an edge bead technique.

To start embossed stitch, pull a threaded needle through the materials at an end point on the design line. String the number of beads that will make up one row, then add one more bead. Sew through the materials at the point on the design line opposite from where you began, then sew back through the material alongside the starting bead of the first row. This pattern creates a long stitch on the backside of the beadwork. As you work, keep your stitches tight; crowding the beads helps to create the three-dimensional embossed effect in the finished piece.

Once the design is beaded, the fabric can be cut to the beaded shape and the edges bound. Fold a ribbon over the edge and stitch it in place. In many pieces, the ribbon is then embellished with a two-bead edge for a more finished look. For details on a two-bead edge see page 107.

Designs for embossed stitch usually followed realistic floral patterns, simple geometric shapes such as circles, and some bird designs (doves are the most common); the completion date was often beaded into the design. Unlike appliqué work where the designs have a lot of detail, embossed designs have very little detail and in a number of pieces the design is really just a shape. Many design motifs resulted from pressure put upon Native artists by the tourists who were purchasing their wares. Whimsies often fall into the category of trinket or knick-knack, with designs that could be beaded quickly—the more whimsies you made, the more money you got.

WRAPPED STITCH

Wrapped stitch was one of the earliest stitches devised by Native Americans after they were introduced to seed beads. It's simple and versatile, and can be regarded as a forerunner of gourd stitch; it was used for many of the same applications, for covering such items as fan handles and awl cases. Wrapped-stitch pieces were created by the Kiowas, Comanches, Sioux—most of the major tribes, in fact.

A piece that is to be embellished with wrapped stitch must first be covered with buckskin so the needle can stitch through to hold the beads in place. Secure the thread by taking a small stitch through the buckskin. String twelve to fifteen beads in color sequence, secure this string in place with a back stitch, and string the next sequence of beads. Proceed in this fashion until the piece is covered.

Holy Mother Earth, the trees and all nature, are witnesses to your thoughts and deeds.

A Winnebago
wise saying

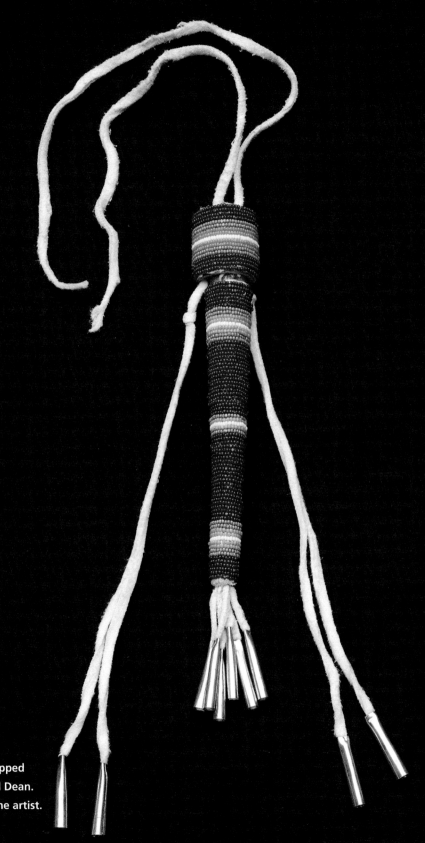

Awl Case. Wrapped
stitched. David Dean.
Collection of the artist.

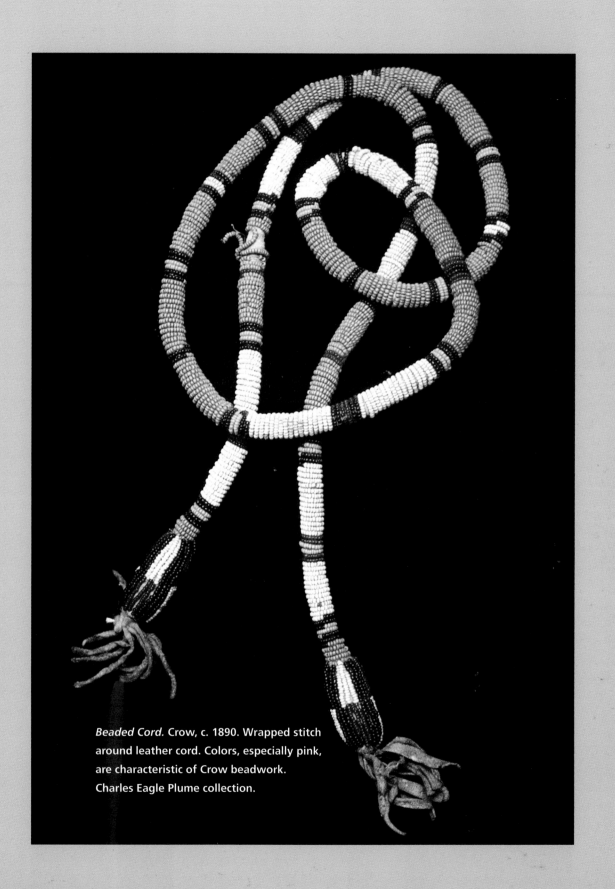

Beaded Cord. Crow, c. 1890. Wrapped stitch around leather cord. Colors, especially pink, are characteristic of Crow beadwork. Charles Eagle Plume collection.

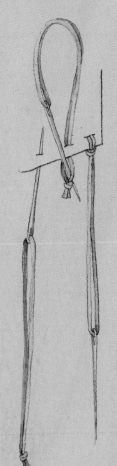

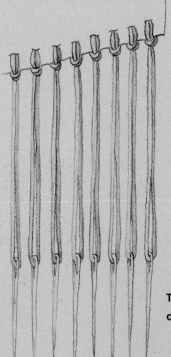

To set up for side stitch, attach the threads to a piece of buckskin with lark's head knots.

The threads should be spaced one bead width apart.

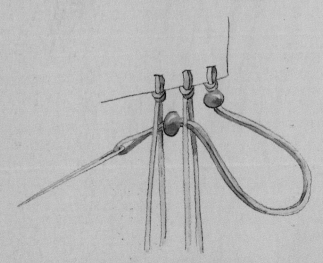

Weave the working thread through sets of threads, leaving one bead between each set.

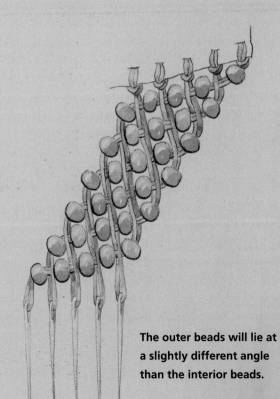

The outer beads will lie at a slightly different angle than the interior beads.

WINNEBEGO SIDE-STITCH BEADWORK

Side-stitch beadwork, also known as diagonal weave and bias weave, can best be described as finger weaving with beads. This technique is one of the most complex used by Native people, and it is possible that it developed after contact with French traders of the late 1700s who were famous for their finger-woven sashes and belts. A regional stitch like embossed stitch, side stitch was used by the Potawatomi, Menominee, Mesquakie, Winnebago, and Osage tribes of the Midwest, and the technique became identified with these same tribes after some were removed to Oklahoma. Historically, side stitch was used to create narrow strips of beadwork that were used for ladies' hair binders, earrings, decorations on cradle boards, and chokers, and it was sometimes done without needles, using coarse horsetail hair as both needle and thread. With this technique, a lot of the thread used is seen, and it is common in historical work to find threads that are a different color than the background (usually red). Due to the number of threads that have to be woven at one time, it is unusual to find side-stitch work over twenty-five beads wide. The method is both complex and time-consuming.

Begin by cutting a small strip of buckskin that is the approximate width of the number of beads that will be woven across the piece. Cut the edge of this strip at a 45-degree angle. Now you must thread a number of needles to equal the number of beads in the width of the finished piece. Thread each needle with a doubled thread and knot the ends. Bring each needle through the angled edge of the buckskin, from back to front, and anchor with a lark's head knot; place the needles one bead width apart.

It is important to use a system that keeps the needles apart and the threads separated. Attaching the buckskin to a piece of Styrofoam with map tacks can do the trick. You can then stick needles into the Styrofoam to keep them out of the way until it is time to weave the threads they hold into the work. The illustrations are oriented for a right-handed beadworker, starting on the right and working to the left. The threads will continually change places, each thread becoming either a warp or a weft as it is woven into place.

Start with the thread on the far right and string the same number of beads as the number of threads that will be woven. Push the first bead into place and thread the needle between the first set of doubled threads to the left (over the first thread and under the second). Push the next bead into place and thread the needle through the next set of doubled threads. Repeat this process until an entire row of beads is in place. When the last bead in the row is pushed into place, you will not have a thread to weave into; the weft thread you are working with now becomes the last warp thread.

Side-stitch pieces can be finished in a number of ways. You may weave the threads back into the beadwork or knot the threads and use them as fringe.

Side-stitch designs can be graphed on the same grid used for loom work, but you must first establish the angle. Once you determine the angle, the designs are easily plotted. Common designs include zigzag lines, floral leaf patterns, geometric designs, and some animal designs.

> Only the mountains and hills live forever, and any day is a good day to die. On battle days, some warriors do not ride the trail back to camp. Instead, they travel over a different road, the spirit trail to the happy hunting grounds beyond the ridge. It is better to die in battle and to be remembered for your brave deeds than to die of old age.
>
> *Iron Hawk 1871*

BEADED EDGINGS AND FINISHING TECHNIQUES

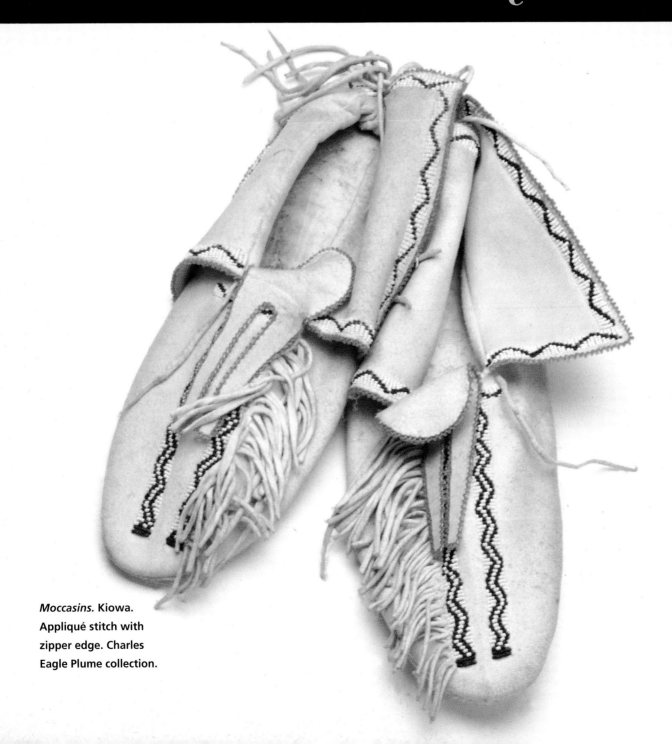

Moccasins. Kiowa. Appliqué stitch with zipper edge. Charles Eagle Plume collection.

Once the beadwork for a project is complete, there often seems to be just a little something missing. That something may be a finished edge. Like fine art work, where the frame makes the picture, so a finished edge makes the beadwork. This chapter offers six types of edges to choose from; many of the techniques presented here follow the process of techniques that have already been discussed. For many beaded pieces, the intended use determines the type of edge needed. Most of the edge work on traditional pieces does not appear to be tribal specific.

SINGLE-BEAD EDGING

Single-bead edging is possibly the simplest form of edge finishing. Anchor a threaded needle through the edge of the item. String a bead, sew through the edge, and pass back through the bead.

TWO-BEAD OR ZIPPER EDGING

Two-bead edging is a simple and elegant way to finish a piece of beadwork. Anchor a threaded needle through the edge of the item. String two beads and pass the needle back through the edge about the space of one bead from the first thread. Pass the needle back through the last bead. This threading causes one bead to lie on its side and one bead to stand up.

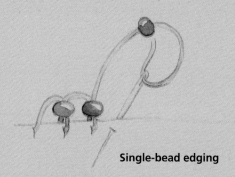

Single-bead edging

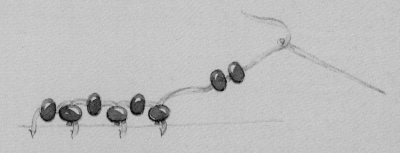

Two-bead or zipper edging

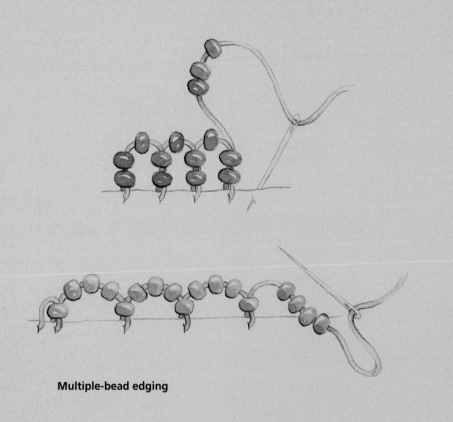

Multiple-bead edging

Rolled-bead edging

MULTIPLE-BEAD EDGING

The same techniques for doing two-bead edging can be used with any number of beads. When you're using more than two beads, increase the spacing between the stitches to make room for the additional beads. The result is an edge of small arches. Depending on the distance between stitches and the number of beads used, different effects can be achieved.

ROLLED-BEAD EDGING

Rolled-bead edgings are generally used with lane-stitch beadwork, particularly on items like cradle boards and pipe bags. The backing for the beadwork needs to be at least an inch longer than the desired finished length of the piece. Work an additional single row of lane stitch about one-half inch from the top edge of the piece. Roll the edge of the backing material toward the back, letting the row of lane stitch form an edge, and stitch the backing to the backside of the work.

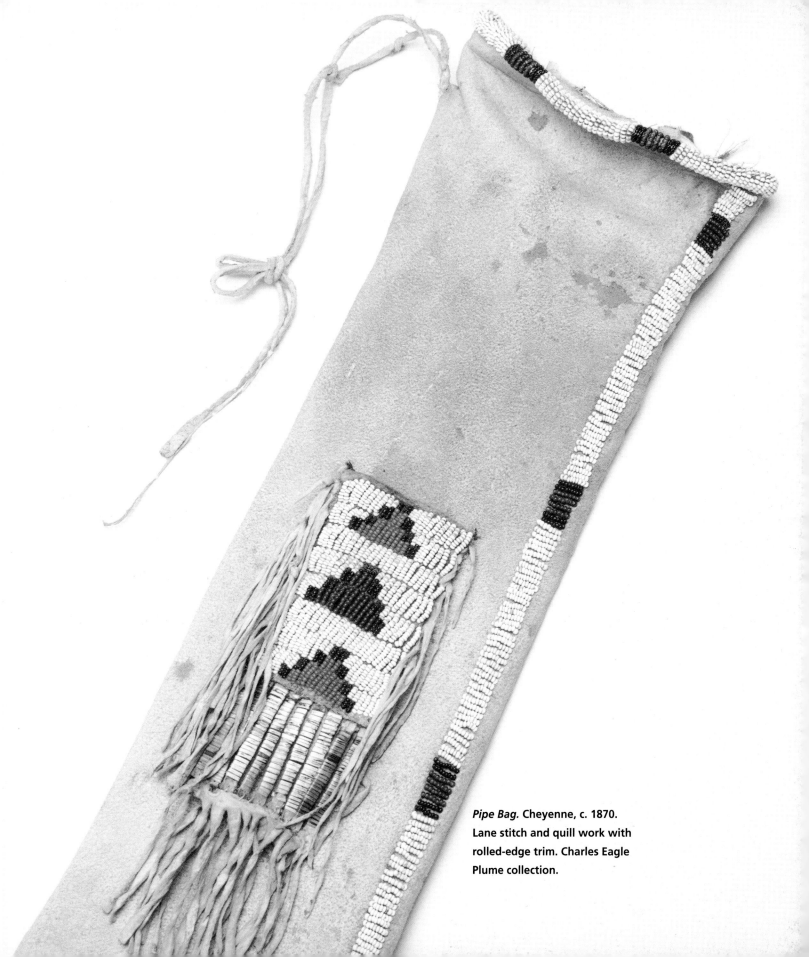

Pipe Bag. Cheyenne, c. 1870.
Lane stitch and quill work with
rolled-edge trim. Charles Eagle
Plume collection.

Rolled-bead edges on flat work

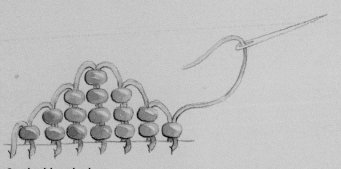

Stacked-bead edge

ROLLED-BEAD EDGES ON FLAT WORK

Rolled-bead edges are commonly found on flat work. This edging is a little different in that it can be used on items such as rosettes and pieces of appliquéd work. Anchor a thread from back to front at the inside edge of the piece. String a few beads, bring them over the edge, and sew back through the piece, bringing the needle out next to the first bead added. When you're doing a rosette with this type of finish, the beads at the very outside edge are spaced a little farther apart than the beads at the inside of the edge.

STACKED-BEAD EDGE

Stacked-bead edges were very popular with the Apache. The first bead is sewn in the same manner as a single-bead edge method. Next, string two beads, sew through the edge, and pass back through both beads. Next, string three beads, sew through the edge, and pass back through the beads. Continue adding one more bead to each row as desired. When you reach the highest row, repeat the process, this time using one less bead on each stitch. The effect is a triangle or half-diamond design.

Bag. Sioux. Lane stitch with
rolled edges. Charles Eagle
Plume collection.

PATTERNS IN NATIVE AMERICAN BEADWORK

Flat Fan. Oklahoma-style design worked in gourd stitch. David Dean, 1998. Collection of the artist.

There's no limit to the patterns that can be worked in the various techniques of Native American beadwork. Native people have always been both creative and adaptive, as you can see by the examples shown throughout this book.

This section provides graph paper suitable for the various techniques that have been discussed, and some sample patterns to get you started. Let this be just the beginning.

Establish a network of fellow beadworkers. This gives you a sounding board for problems that occur and gives you someone who can help you improve your work through constructive advice based on knowledge of the problem.

David Dean

LANE STITCH

Any design that can be worked in narrow bands or "lanes" is suitable for this versatile stitch. Sometimes angles and curves are introduced against a background of solid parallel lanes.

The earth is the mother of all people, and all people should have equal rights upon it.

Chief Joseph, 1879

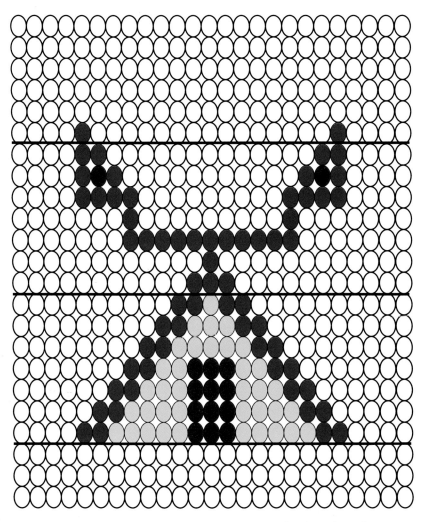

This design is typical of the second lane-stitch design phase, from about 1840 to about 1870.

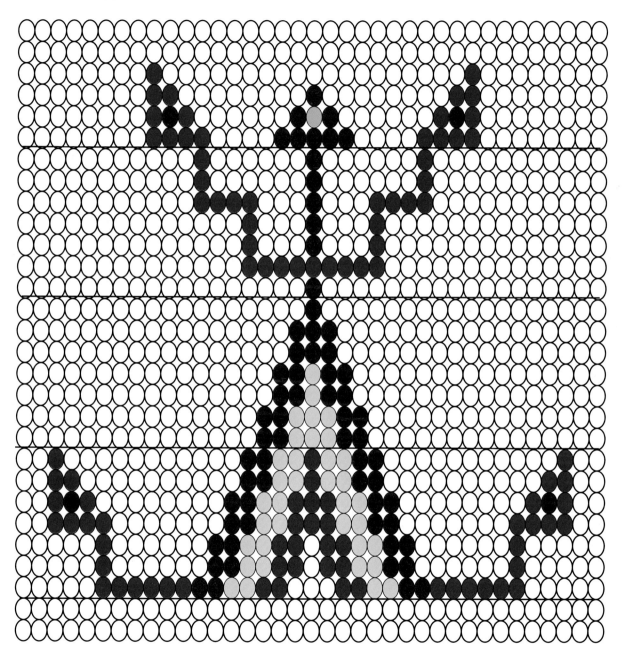

New lines were added to lane-stitch designs during the second phase of development.

Chalk white remained the predominant background color for lane-stitch designs during the mid-1800s.

Designs with small lines and triangles became common during the second phase of lane-stitch design development.

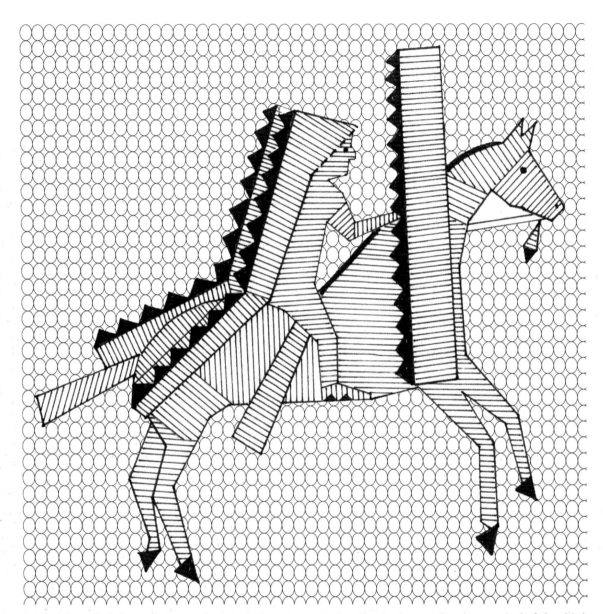

Pictorial motifs in lane stitch are often worked against a chalk-white background and are typical of the third phase of lane-stitch design.

LOOM BEADWORK

The same graphed patterns can be worked on either heddle or tension looms.

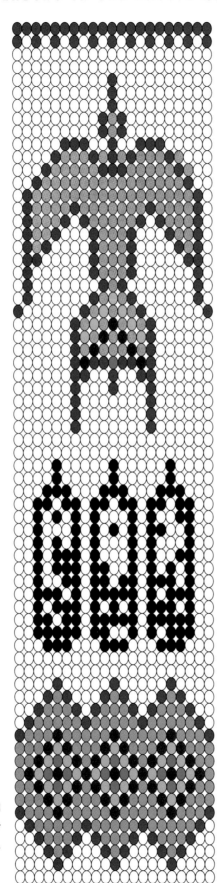

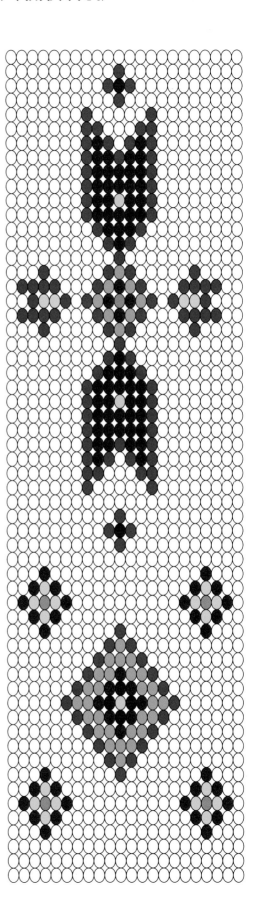

These designs may be used for belts, dance clothes, or other flat items.

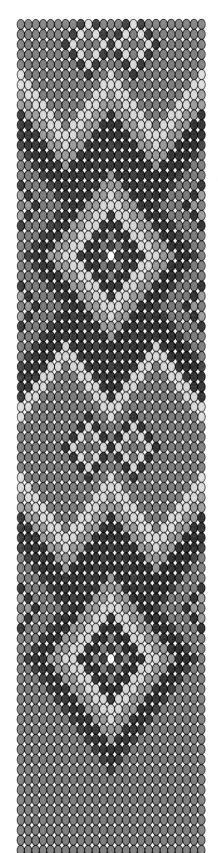

Bold geometric shapes are typical in Pan-Indian-style loom work.

The life of the Indian is like the wings of the air. That is why you notice the hawk knows how to get his prey. The Indian is like that. The hawk swoops down on its prey; so does the Indian. In his lament he is like an animal. For instance, the coyote is sly; so is the Indian. The eagle the same. That is why the Indian is always feathered up; he is a relative to the wings of the air.

Black Elk, Oglala Sioux 1891

Chippewa bandoleer design for a heddle loom. These designs are thought to have been inspired by the Persian rugs that were popular from 1875 to 1920.

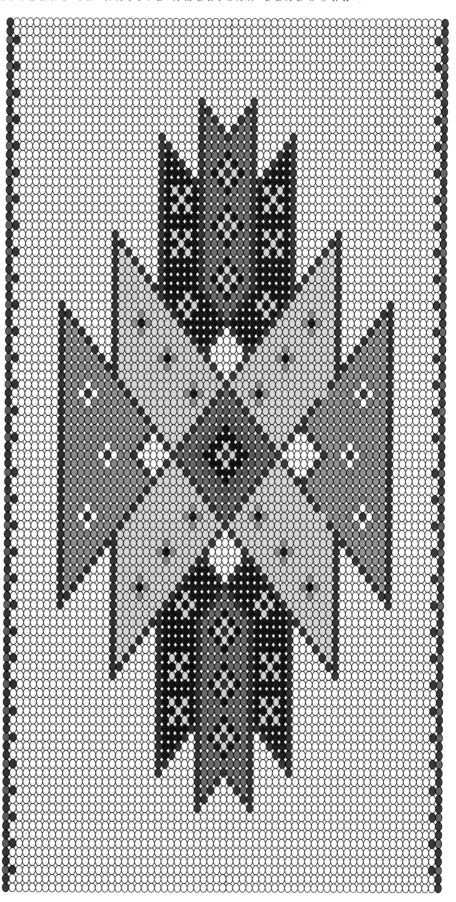

Center design on a Pan-Indian-style belt. Most belts are designed with a strong middle pattern and weaker designs on each end. When this pattern is beaded with 13° cut beads, the final width is 3¾".

APPLIQUÉ

Any design can be worked in versatile appliqué stitch, from geometrics to curvilinear images from nature to boldly patterned symmetrical rosettes. Abstract floral designs may be split in half or quartered. Each half or quarter is then beaded in a different color.

Out of the Indian approach to life there came a great freedom—an intense and absorbing love for nature; a respect for life; enriching faith in a Supreme Power; and principles of truth, honesty, generosity, equity, and brotherhood as a guide to mundane relations.

Luther Standing Bear, Oglala Sioux

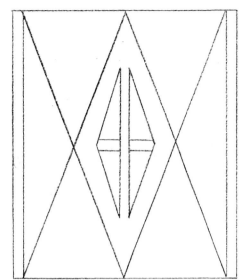

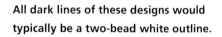

All dark lines of these designs would
typically be a two-bead white outline.

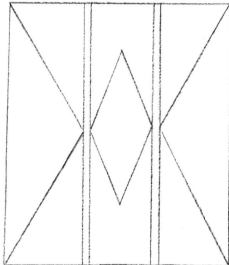

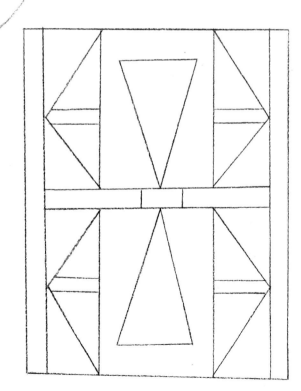

Pictorial designs taken from nature lend themselves
well to appliqué.

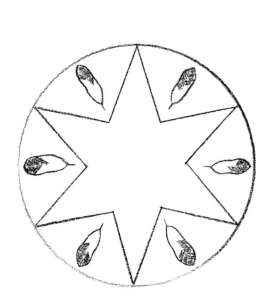

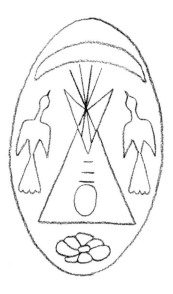

Rosettes (above and above right) often start with a single bead sewn down in the center, surrounded by a row of return stitch. They are then completed in two-needle appliqué.

GOURD STITCH

The way each row of beads is offset by a half-bead from the previous row makes gourd stitch especially appropriate for designs with strong verticals and diagonals.

Eagle Feathers

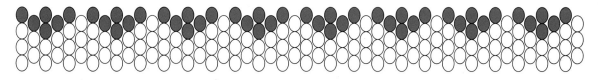

Half Diamond

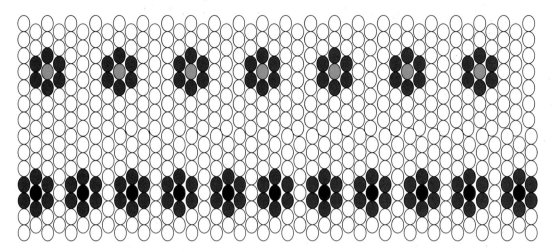

Flowers

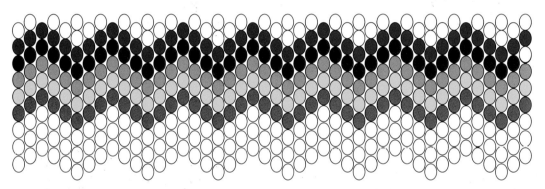

Zigzag

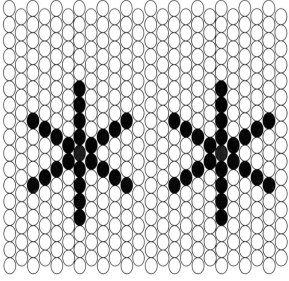

Stars

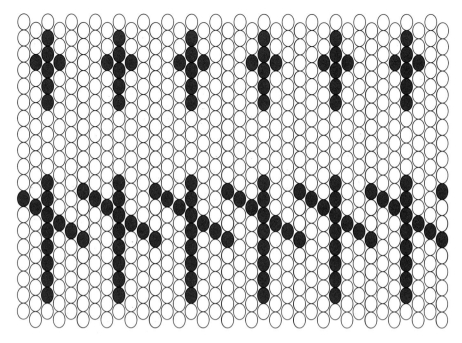

Crosses

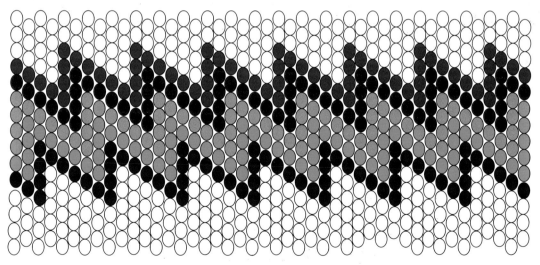

Saw Tooth

Spider Webs

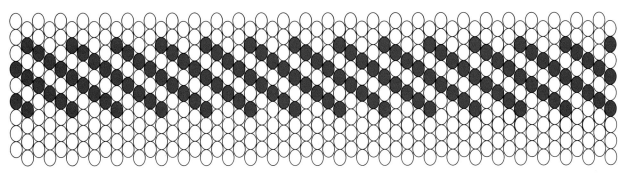

Barber Pole

Straight Lines

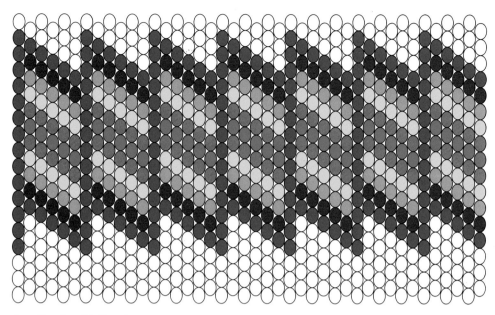

Saw Tooth with Panels

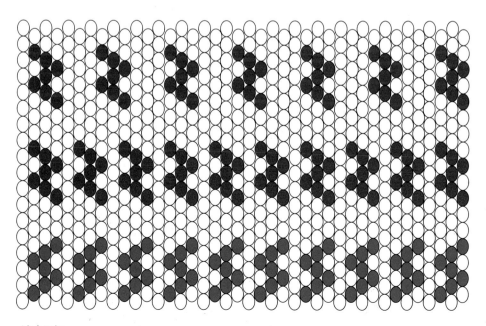

Lightning

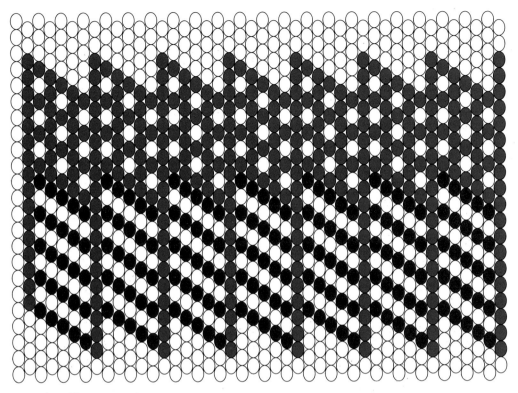

American Flags

Zigzag with Panels

THREE-DROP GOURD STITCH

This technique is unique to Native American beadwork. Design units are six beads wide.
It has a stronger diagonal slant than regular gourd stitch.

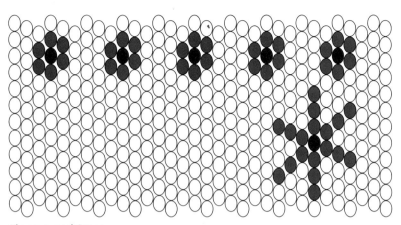

Flowers and Stars

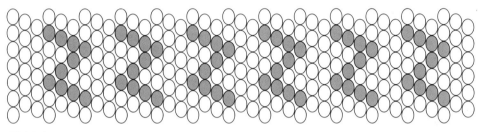

Lightning

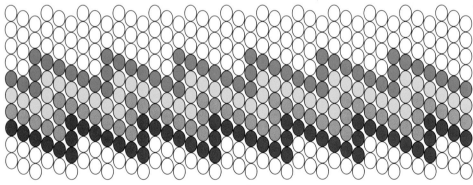

Saw Tooth

Half -Diamonds

American Flags

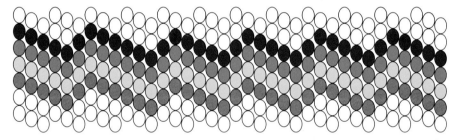

Zigzag

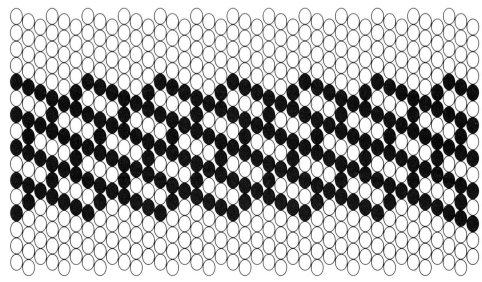

Spider Web

COMANCHE BRICK STITCH

The same patterns that work well for gourd stitch are appropriate for Comanche brick stitch. The difference is that the same motif will be slightly flattened in brick stitch, and vertically elongated in gourd stitch.

COMANCHE BRICK STITCH

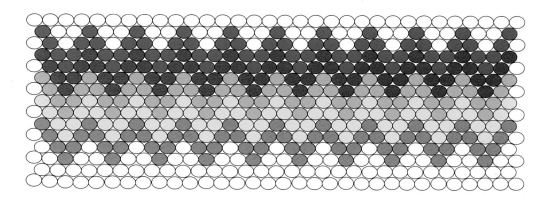

Zigzag

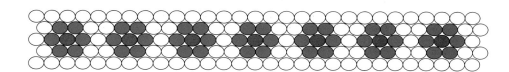

Flowers

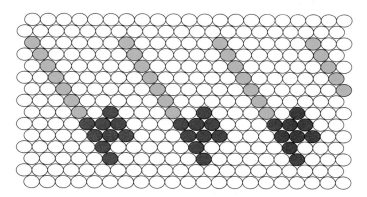

Peace Pipe

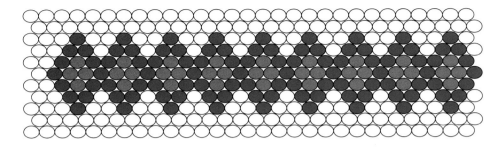

Diamonds

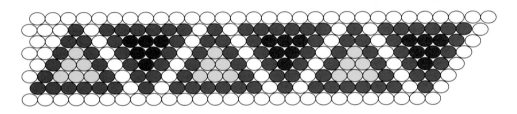

Reversed Triangle

Spider Web

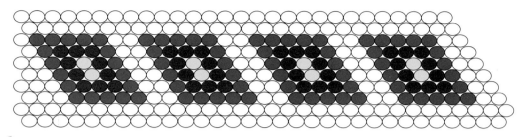

Squares

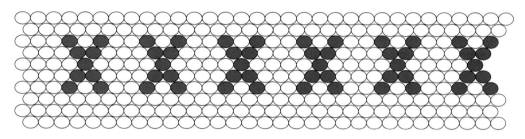

"X" Pattern

Chevron

Stars

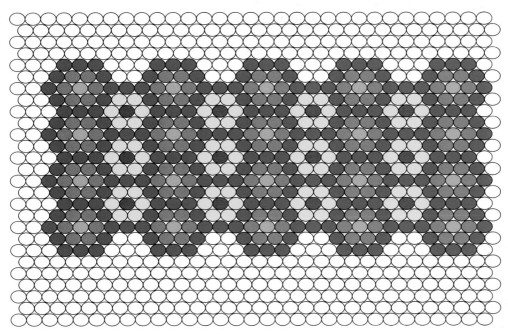

Chicken Wire Pattern

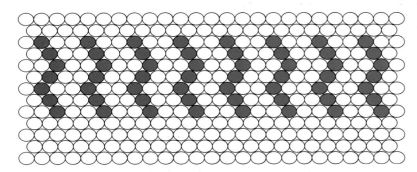

Lightning Bolts

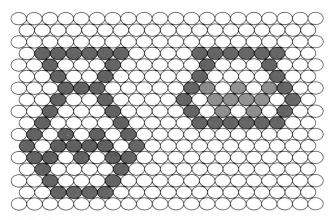

Pot Design

Interlocking Diamonds

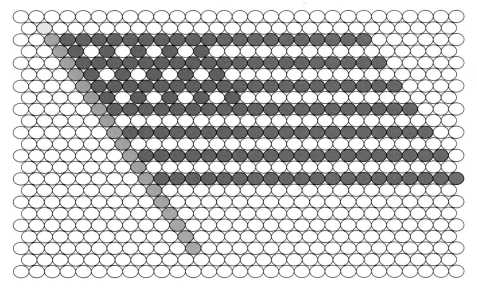

Flag

SIDE STITCH

In this beaded variation of finger-weaving, the beads are aligned diagonally, and the beginning and ending edges are slanted. Twenty-five beads is a typical limit for width.

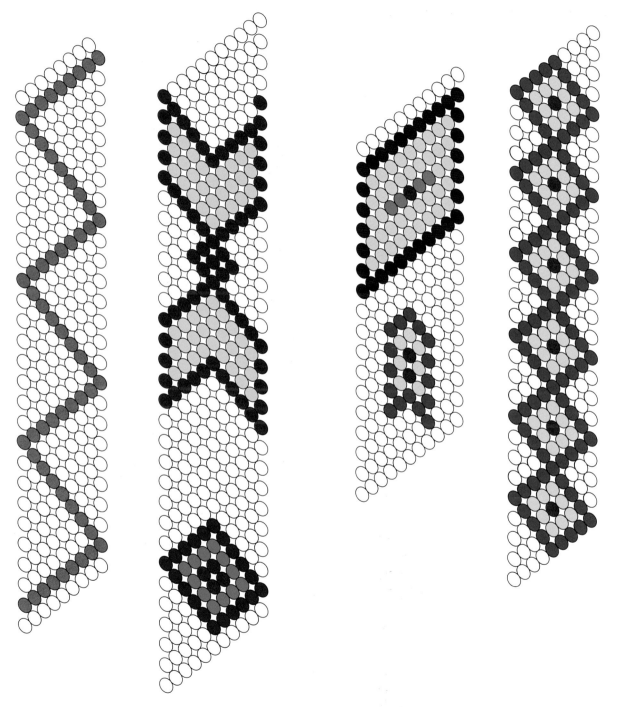

A design grid can be made using loom beadwork paper cut at an angle.

BIBLIOGRAPHY

The following is a list of museum catalogs, books, and magazines that offer good photos of beadwork. Some of the beadwork is contemporary and some is historical. Also included on this list are a number of resources for beadwork instruction. When you're viewing the photos in these resources, use a good magnifying glass so that you can observe the finest details.

BOOKS AND CATALOGS

Aikman, Susanne. *A Primer: The Art of Native American Beadwork*. Denver, Colorado: Morning Flower Press, 1980.

Alden, Jill. *Contemporary American Indian Beadwork: The Exquisite Art*. New York: Dolph Publishing, 1999.

Baldwin, John. *Early Knives & Beaded Sheaths*. West Olive, Michigan: Early American Artistry-Trading Company, 1997.

Barth, Georg J. *Native American Beadwork*. Stevens Point, Wisconsin: Richard C. Schneider Publishing, 1993.

Bebbington, Julia M. *Quillwork of the Plains*. Calgary, Alberta: Glenbow Alberta Institute, 1982.

Bradford, C. J., and Thom Laine. *Dancing Colors*. San Francisco: McQuiston & Partners Inc., 1992.

Brundl, Heiz. *Myothos Wild West: Die Sammbung Brundl, The Brundl Collection*. Berlin, Germany: Hudson Bay Trading Post & Winnoa Gmbh, 1999.

Coe, Ralph, ed. *Sacred Circles*. Kansas City, Missouri: Nelson Gallery of Art and Atkins Museum of Fine Art, 1976.

Conn, Richard. *Circles of the World*. Denver, Colorado: Denver Art Museum, 1982.

Dean, David. *Native Pockets*. Galesburg, Illinois: Heirloom Originals, 1998.

———. *Craft of the Mind, Art of the Soul: Beadwork Techniques of Native American Indians*. Galesburg, Illinois: Heirloom Originals, 1997.

DeLange, Deon. *Techniques of Beading Earrings*. Ogden, Utah: Eagle View Publishing, 1938.

———. *More Techniques of Beading Earrings*. Ogden, Utah: Eagle View Publishing, 1938.

Dubin, Louis Sherr. *North American Indian Jewelry and Design*. New York: Harry N. Abrams Publishers, 1999.

———. *The History of Beads*. New York: Harry N. Abrams Publishers, 1987.

Dutton, E. P. *American Indian Art: Form and Tradition*. New York: Walker Art Center and The Minneapolis Institute of Art, 1972.

Ewers, John. *Blackfeet Crafts*. Stevens Point, Wisconsin: Richard C. Schneider Publishing, 1986.

Goodhue, Horace R. *Indian Bead-Weaving Patterns*. St. Paul, Minnesota: Bead Craft, 1989.

Hail, Barbara A. *Hau,Kola*. Bristol, Rhode Island: Haffenreffer Museum of Anthropology, 1980.

Hanson, James. *Spirits in the Arts*. Kansas City, Missouri: The Lowell Press, 1994.

Heinbuch, Jean. *A Beadwork Companion*. Ogden, Utah: Eagle View Publishing.

Hensler, Christy Ann. *Guide to Indian Quillwork*. Surrey, British Columbia: Hancock House, 1989.

Herbst, Toby, and Joel Kopp. *The Flag in American Indian Art*. Cooperstown, New York: New York Historical Association, 1993.

Hobbs, Torrence, and Robert Hobbs. *Art of the Red Earth People: The Mesquakie of Iowa*. Ames, Iowa: University of Iowa Museum of Art, 1989.

Hodge, G. Stuart. *The American Indian: The American Flag*. Flint, Michigan: Flint Institute, 1975.

Hungry Wolf, Adolph and Beverly. *Blackfoot Craftworker's Book*. Skookumchuck, British Columbia: Good Medicine Books, 1977.

Hunt, Ben W., and J. F. "Buck" Burshears. *American Indian Beadwork*. Milwaukee, Wisconsin: Bruce Miller Publishing, 1951.

Isaac, Barbara. *Hall of the North American Indian*. Cambridge, Massachusetts: Peabody Museum Press, 1990.

Lomahjaftewa, Gloria A. *Glass Tapestry*. Phoenix, Arizona: The Heard Museum, 1993.

Lyford, Carrie A. *Iroquois Crafts*. Stevens Point, Wisconsin: Richard C. Schneider Publishing, 1982.

———. *Ojibwa Crafts*. Stevens Point, Wisconsin: Richard C. Schneider Publishing, 1982.

———. *Quill and Beadwork of the Western Sioux*. Boulder, Colorado: Johnson Publishing, 1940.

Marrow, Mabel. *Indian Rawhide*. Norman, Oklahoma: University of Oklahoma Press, 1975.

Miller, Preston. *Four Winds Indian Beadwork & Old Flathead Photos*. St. Ignatiris, Montana: Mission Valley News, 1971.

Miller, Preston, and Carolyn Corey. *The Four Winds Guide to Indian Trade Goods and Replicas*. Atglen, Pennsylvania: Scheffler Publishing, 1998.

———. *The Four Winds Guide to Indian Artifacts*. Atglen, Pennsylvania: Scheffler Publishing, 1997.

Monroe, Dan L. *Gifts of the Spirit*. Salem, Massachusetts: Exhibition of the Peabody Essex Museum, Acme Printing, 1996.

Monture, Joel. *The Complete Guide to Traditional Native American Beadwork*. New York: Collier Books, 1993.

Olsen, Gordon L. *Beads: Their Use by Upper Great Lakes Indians*. Grand Rapids, Minnesota: Grand Rapids Public Museum, 1979.

Orchard, William C. *Beads and Beadwork of the American Indian*. New York: La Salle Litho Corp., 1975.

Penney, David W. *Art of the American Indian Frontier*. Vancouver, British Columbia: Douglas & McIntryre, 1992.

Penney, David W., and George C. Longfish. *Native American Art*. New York: Hugh Lauter Levin Associates Inc., 1994.

Schmidt, Jeremy, and Thom Laine. *Dolls & Toys of Native Americans*. San Francisco: McQuistion & McQuistion, 1995.

Scriver, Bob. *The Blackfeet: Artist of the Northern Plains*. Kansas City, Missouri: The Lowell Press, 1990.

Smith, Monte. *The Technique of North American Indian Beadwork*. Odgen, Utah: Eagle View Publishing.

Sommer, Langley. *Native American Art*. New York: Smithmark Publishing, 1994.

Struever, Martha Hopkins. *Bags of Friendship: Bandolier Bags of the Great Lakes Indians*. Santa Fe, New Mexico: Morning Star Gallery, 1996.

Swan, Daniel C. *Peyote Religious Art*. Jackson, Mississippi: University of Mississippi Press, 1999.

Taylor, Colin F. *The Native Americans*. New York: Smithmark Publishing, 1991.

———. *Buckskin and Buffalo*. England: Emirates Press, 1998.

Thom, Laine. *In The Spirit of Mother Earth*. San Francisco: McQuistion & McQuistion, 1994.

———. *Becoming Brave*. San Francisco: McQuistion & Partners Inc. 1992.

Walker, James R. *Akicita*. Lincoln, Nebraska: University of Nebraska Press, 1983.

Walters, Anna Lee. *The Spirit of Native America*. San Francisco: McQuiston & Partners, 1989.

Walton, Ann T. *After the Buffalo Were Gone*. St. Paul Minnisota: Sexton Printing, 1985.

Weldschut, William, and John C. Ewers. *Crow Indian Beadwork*. Ogden, Utah: Eagle View Publishing, 1985.

White, George. *Craft Manual of Northwest Indian Beading*. Ronan, Montana: George White, 1971.

White, Mary. *How to do Beadwork*. Mineola, New York: Dover Publishing, 1972.

Wissler, Clark. *North American Beadwork Design*. Mineola, New York: Dover Publishing, 1919.

Woerpel, Loren, and Donna Woerpel. *Beadworking with Today's Materials*. Escanaba, Michigan: Johnston Printing and Offset, 1989.

Wolf, Gray. *American Beadwork Design*. New York: Plume Trading Co., 1951.

Wooley, David. *Eye of the Angel*. Northampton, Massachusetts: White Star Press, 1990.

Wordwell, Allen. *Native Paths: American Indian Art of the Charles and Valerie Diker Collection*. East Greenwich, Rhode Island: Meridian Printing Co, 1998.

Wright, Jesse G. *Native American Art at the Philbrook*. Tulsa, Oklahoma: Philbrook Museum of Art, 1980.

Magazine Articles

Bates, Craig, D. "Beadwork of the Far West." *Moccasin Tracks*, Vol. 6, #6, pp 6–8.

Brewer, Bob. "Crow Blanket Strip and Crow Stitch." *Moccasin Tracks*, Vol. 9, #7, pp 10–12.

Bugelski, Peter. "Lazy Stitch Beadwork." *Whispering Winds*, Vol. 10, #8 pp 8–9.

Chandler, Milford, and David Kracinski. "Unusual Beadwork Techniques, Part 1." *American Indian Tradition*, Vol. 8, #5.

———. "Unusual Beadwork Techniques, Part 2." *American Indian Tradition*, Vol. 9, #1.

Chronister, Allen. "Arapaho Beadwork." *Whispering Winds*, Vol. 23, #6, pp 10–12.

Conn, Dick. "Beadwork With Style." *American Indian Hobbyist*, Vol. 6, #7 and 8.

———. "Cheyenne Style Beadwork." *American Indian Hobbyist*, Vol. 7, #2.

Cooley, Jim. "The Abstract Floral Clout." *Moccasin Tracks*, Vol. 10, #9, pp 4–11.

———. "Beaded Bolo Ties." *Moccasin Tracks*, Vol. 9, #7, pp 10–14.

Johnson, Mike. "Floral Beadwork in North America." *American Indian Crafts and Culture*, Vol. 7, #9, pp 6–11.

Lotter, John. "Heddle Loom Beadwork." *American Indian Crafts and Culture*, Vol. 7, #7, pp 2–7.

Nimerfro, Steve. "Sioux Lazy Stitch." *Moccasin Tracks*, Vol. 7, #7, pp 6–7.

Salzer, Robert. "Central Algonkin Beadwork" *American Indian Tradition*, Vol. 7, #5.

Smith, Jerry. "Mounting a Loom Beaded Belt." *Moccasin Tracks*, Vol. 10, #8, pp 8–9.

———. "Edge Beadwork Plus." *Moccasin Tracks*, Vol. 7, #4, p 13.

———. "Shawl Dance Beadwork." *Moccasin Tracks*, Vol. 6, #9, pp 8–9.

———. "Comanche Style Net Beadwork." *Moccasin Tracks*, Vol.5, #8, p 12.

Smith, Jerry, and Scott Sutton. "Beaded Barrettes." *Moccasin Tracks*, Vol. 6, #5, pp 8–11.

Sutton, Scott. "Beaded Medallions." *Moccasin Tracks*, Vol. 8, #2, pp 6–10.

Stewart, Tyrone. "Peyote Beadwork: Part 1." *Singing Wire*, Vol. 3, #1, pp 3–6.

———. Tyrone. "Peyote Beadwork: Part 2." *American Indian Crafts and Culture*, Vol. 3, #9, pp 3–6.

Stone, Ben. "Applique Beadwork." *American Indian Crafts and Culture*, Vol. 5, # 1, pp 5–7.

Vonbonk, Hermann. "An Early Beadwork Technique of the Plains Indians." *American Indian Crafts and Culture*, Vol. 6, #4, pp 7–8.

Walker, Bill, and Anita Walker. "Rosettes." *Whispering Winds*, Vol. 22, #3, pp 7–12.

Wall, Sam. "Beading Rosettes." *Whispering Winds*, Vol. 8, #9, pp 8–10.

———. "Loom Beadwork." *Whispering Winds*, Vol. 5, #5, pp 8–9.

Other Sources

Crow Indian Art: Papers Presented to the Crow Art Symposium. Mission, South Dakota: Chandler Institution, 1984.

How to Bead Native American Style video series. Sandy Rhoades and Scott Swearingen, producers. Volume 1, Loom Beadwork; Volume 2, Lazy Stitch Beadwork; Volume 3, Peyote Beadwork; Volume 4, Medallions: Running Stitch Beadwork; Volume 5, Two-Needle Applique Beadwork. Tulsa, Oklahoma: Full Circle Communications.

Morning Star Gallery: Vols. 1–6, buyer's catalog. Santa Fe, New Mexico.

Sherwood's Spirits of America: Vol.1, buyer's catalog. Santa Fe, New Mexico.

INDEX